Impressive Reviews & Recommendations ....

"Patrick Tinney has created a very readable book (Unlocking Yes Sales Negotiation Lessons & Strategy) that integrates the art and science of negotiation with his views on improving the sales process. Tinney shares the experience he has gained in a book that flows from his approach on the philosophy and process of negotiation through to key strategies to pursue. The reader can keep referring back to the book time and time again. Each chapter is concise and explains the why and how, often with a personal experience that provides context. Patrick's personal style and genuine passion for the process comes through. His viewpoint blends the short term objectives of the deal with the long term view of the relationship at stake. This is not a textbook but a philosophical and strategic approach developed through decades of high profile negotiation mostly in the high stakes world of advertising. Regardless of the business or organization where you work, this book is well worth your time to understand how to prepare and work through a successful negotiation."

Steve Macfarlane
Director of Sales, Trader Corporation, Toronto, ON, Canada

"A power house of Negotiation Strategies and Advice. Unlocking Yes has quickly become one of my few go to books when closing a new deal. Well written and full of advice for the sales and marketing professional."

Christopher Kata
CIO, Axiom Real-Time Metrics, Toronto, ON, Canada

"If selling is the art of negotiating Unlocking YES is what comfort food is to the masses. Unlocking YES is the full meal deal. Unlocking Yes is easy to read and digest which makes it palpable for any sales person to learn the correct behaviors essential to making money. Unlocking Yes helps sales people to reinvent themselves. Sales is the last God given frontier to making unlimited income requiring no other talent than intrinsic motivation and Unlocking YES."

Paul Tessier
President – CEO, Chief Executive Optimalist
Rope Access Maintenance (RAM), Saint John, NB, Canada

D1301439

"In today's fiercely competitive marketplace, superior sales negotiations and strategies positively impact proposals and ultimately company performance. Patrick has assembled a valuable one-stop resource providing real-life lessons that explores the disciplines needed to build trust, navigate objections and close deals."

Bruce C. Roher
Partner, Fuller Landau LLP, Chartered Professional Accountants, Toronto, Canada

"Patrick has taken some of most complex human interactions and skillfully explained strategy in very simple and understandable terms (in Unlocking Yes Sales Negotiation Lessons & Strategy I have been in sales all my life, and I wish I had this book 20 years ago. Planning before, during, and after negotiations would have been smoother and more lucrative. I also get a sense that Patrick is a very ethical man – his sales techniques are not out to gauge the buyer, they are designed to meet the needs of both buyer and seller. But there's something else: This is an excellent book for sales forces, large and small. I believe it is also a book for people in all walks of life, not just for those who can technically call themselves sales people. The need for negotiation skills is not limited to when there is money on the table or an occasion to haggle over a price, product, or service. Every business person who has a boss, a co-worker, or an employee can become more effective when selling innovative ideas, asking for a raise, selling corporate strategy within the walls of your own company, and so much more. Every entrepreneur needs to incorporate Patrick's principles when raising seed funding and further rounds of funding. And dare I say that anyone who has ever been a parent, a spouse or a friend would benefit from the life principles in this book. Get the book. It's a keeper."

Mary Jo Krump
Social Media Director, The Purpose is Profit, Centennial, CO, USA

"Unlocking Yes" will be a great resource to sales and marketing professionals. The author has managed to create a resource guide that has the credibility of a text book combined with real life stories to illustrate all the key messages."

Glenn Marshall
President, Greening Marketing Inc., Hamilton, ON, Canada

UNLOCKING YES

Sales Negotiation

Lessons & Strategy

UNLOCKING YES

Sales Negotiation

Lessons & Strategy

Patrick Tinney

2014

First Printing: 2014

ISBN 978-0-9938284-16

Centroid Publishing
STN Main, 150 King Street P.O. Box 713
Peterborough, Ontario, Canada K9J 6Z8
www.centroidmarketing.com

Ordering Information:

Special discounts are available on quantity purchases by corporations, associations, educators, and others. For details, contact the publisher at the above listed address.

U.S. trade bookstores and wholesalers: Please contact
Centroid Publishing   Tel: 1-705-657-2518
Email: patrick@centroidmarketing.com

DEDICATION

To my Family

Jean Tinney-Zemelis
Barbara Tinney
Connie Tinney
Sean Tinney

Your ability to persevere and overcome life's obstacles
will always be a beacon of light to me.

CONTENTS

INTRODUCTION 1

PART I – PHILOSOPHY 3
1   Today's Economy and the Negotiation Marathon 4
2   Why Consultative Selling Integrates With   Negotiation Planning 7
3   Good, Better, Best Negotiator 10
4   Create a Philosophy 13
5   How Effectively Does Your Sales Team Negotiate? 16
6   Ten Winning Sales Negotiator Traits 19
7   Four Powerful Words 22
8   Supercharge Your Sales Negotiation 25

PART II - Exploration 29
9   High Value Questions…Invaluable 30
10 "Us & Them"…Ten Important Questions 33
11 Profit Through Disciplined Listening 36
12 True Genius In Reconnaissance 39
13 Brand Alignment And Its Influences In A Sales   Negotiation 42
14 Define Objectives. Negotiate Like A Pro 45
15 Cash Is King…The Buyer's Market 48
16 Power SWOT Before Major Sales Negotiations 51
17 SWOT Competitors Before Negotiations 54
18 SWOT Your Customer Before A Sales Negotiation 57

PART III - Relationships & Trust 60
19 Building Trust 61
20 Relationships Matter 64
21 E.Q. Versus I.Q. in Sales Negotiation 67
22 Reduce Stress…Save Energy 70
23 Reduce Conflict…Focus On The End Game 73
24 Smartly Withdrawing From A Sales Negotiation 76
25 The Value Of Storytelling 78
26 Tips For Handling Aggressive Negotiators 82
27 Sales Negotiation Traps To Avoid 86

PART IV - Preparing To Close 89
28 From Better To Best 90
29 Why BATNA Is Such A Powerful Tool 93
30 Opportunity Sales Objections 95
31 Sales Negotiations, Plus Time, Equals More Money 98
32 Navigate The Bargaining Continuum 101
33 Use Smart Sales Negotiation Tactics 104
34 Beware Of Leaky Strategies 107
35 Negotiation Strategy…Is One Enough? 110
36 Limited Strategies Lead To Less Profit 112
37 The Importance Of Framing Sales Negotiations 115
38 Be Creative When Weak 118
39 Negotiating Via Mobile, Skype Or E-Mail 122
40 Negotiation Tips For Women In Business 125

PART V - The Close 128
41 Managing Risk 129
42 Powerful Scripting and Un-Scripting 132
43 Credibility At The Negotiation Table Pays 135
44 Effective Trial Closes 138
45 Win More With Value Statements 141
46 Smartly Navigate Price Traps 144
47 Identifying And Navigating An Impasse 147

PART VI - The Aftermath 150
48 The Value Of Post Mortem In Negotiations 151

PART VII - 12 Negotiation Strategies 154
12 Buyer Negotiation Strategies Sellers Need To Know 154
Strategy Summary 167

FINAL THOUGHTS 168
ACKNOWLEDGEMENTS 169
REFERENCES 170
INDEX 171

INTRODUCTION

Sales negotiation is an integral part of consultative selling. Interestingly, the academic and the business communities seem at odds as to how to marry these two subjects.

If you are reading this book, you are seeking constructive methods to bring strong relationship-based selling to profitable closure. In *Unlocking Yes,* we offer a series of real-life lessons, business cases, business vignettes, tactics, and strategies to help the reader make solid decisions in negotiating wise deals that stand the test of time.

I have specifically written *Unlocking Yes* to address the bargaining needs of sales professionals. Our mission is to provide you with strong examples of how to engage professional buyers who are well-schooled in procurement processes and negotiation practices that are systematic and cultural. This will enable sales professionals to bring relationship-based selling to profitable closures.

As a sales negotiator with decades of experience, I will always be a bigger-piece-of-the-pie negotiator. I look for the best sales negotiation solutions available for my customers. My caveat is that these solutions must be profitable or provide a gateway to wider profit in a measurable period of time.

Unlocking Yes will do its best to be a long-term road map for sales negotiators of all stripes. We will discuss and illustrate sales negotiation as an end-to-end thought process that is integral to successful consultative selling.

Your customers are professional buyers. Let's work together in *Unlocking Yes* to reveal the information you need to know to make you an accomplished, profitable sales negotiator who is prepared to intelligently engage the best procurement and buying professionals in your sales category.

Unlocking Yes is written sequentially to provide context to the process of sales negotiation. I have used the phrases "Sales Negotiation" and "Business Negotiation" in this book interchangeably for effect.

Patrick Tinney

As you read through *Unlocking Yes*, be introspective and look for the pieces of this book that you can incorporate into your sales negotiation world right away.

I'm pleased to share these life lessons and negotiation strategies with you.

Here's to making and saving money!

PART I – PHILOSOPHY

1

TODAY'S ECONOMY AND THE NEGOTIATION MARATHON

We are six years into the Great Recession, and sales negotiation has never been tougher.

You'd have to look back to World War II or the Great Depression to see the kind of wealth destruction we have witnessed globally.

Today, we stand with nearly unprecedented consumer debt in North America. The U.S.A. is still bouncing in and out of recession-like economic conditions. It is estimated that there is as much as $1.3 trillion dollars of unspent capital expenditure budgets lying dormant on North American corporate balance sheets. Corporations want to make money but, do not want to spend money. Some businesses have resorted to shrinking the size of their operations to fit their declining revenues. Topline sales growth is a guessing game for many companies.

Lenders are still cautious about who can borrow and how much they will lend. The market is also facing a big drop in consumer confidence and retail demand.

Truly, a whole slew of ill-timed economic chickens coming to roost all at the same time.

There are signs of economic improvement. But, it's masked by the billions of dollars of government liquidity and quantitative easing being injected into financial systems around the world.

Business contract negotiations have been extremely challenging with too many sellers chasing too few buyers. This indicates we are in the clutches of a buyer's market, and the buyers know they have the upper hand. Rather than being an annual affair, it seems customers of all stripes want to negotiate everything on a weekly basis. So what is your company doing to grow your topline sales and protect precious margins in this negotiation marathon?

We are all short of time; it doesn't matter whether you are selling or buying. With global business running 24 hours a day, greater demands on all business people, and the impact of technology (both good and bad), time is truly compressed. Vendors need to sell more, while buyers take more time to research, consider, and decide on their best options. As such, time compression reveals a fairly noticeable drop in civility. With so little time and so many changes in our current marketplace, we need to raise our game or have a competitor eat our breakfast.

Throw your own spin on your company's competitive and economic realities, and now you *really* get the picture.

Here are a few things that I would really like you to key in on:

1)   Learn the value of asking the best questions possible. This will save you time and turn ordinary customer engagements into power calls.

2)   All of us are in the relationship business. Relationships are the tipping point for business stability, sales growth and negotiation profitability. Customer relationships are critical.

3)   Collect customer intelligence on a weekly basis and especially before a negotiation begins. Do this through casual conversations and regular meetings and not necessarily pertaining to the negotiation. In other words, get the other side to talk about their world – their company goals, growth expectations or competitive challenges.

4) The above will allow your side to do a mini SWOT Analysis (Strengths, Weaknesses, Opportunities and Threats) of the other side and their and your competitors.

5) Be creative. Customers want creative ideas not stuff. Stuff gets negotiated as a commodity. Beware.

6) Think strategy. Too many of us want to jump into negotiations without a game plan and the results are not always what we had hoped for. Try to grow your understanding of strategy mixed with crafty tactics that will give you flexibility under pressure.

7) Understand the importance of BATNA (Best Alternative To A Negotiated Agreement). A BATNA is a stream of plans and back up plans.

8) Learn and understand the power of handling objections under pressure. This is a magnificent skill and one that will turn negativity into surprisingly quick customer driven closes.

9) Close smart deals. Think about all of your negotiations as having the basis for potential longevity.

10) Finally, be critical of your own work. Tear apart every deal you complete and look for improvement. Sales negotiation is a process but, it is also an art form.

Even with all of this groundwork, you are just at the entry point (believe it, or not) where you can start asking probing, armor piercing questions of the other side that will build your case in preparation for the negotiating marathon.

2

WHY CONSULTATIVE SELLING INTEGRATES WITH NEGOTIATION PLANNING

Sellers are always looking for more effective ways to grow relationships with their important customers. Gone are the days when a salesperson could just pick up the phone and get a quick appointment.

Increasingly, customers are barricading themselves behind gatekeepers and virtual e-mail walls. Customers are only inviting into their inner circle suppliers with whom they have a history or in whom they see great potential. On this note, consultative selling is essential for sellers who have to be close to their customers. Consultative selling in this context is trust and collaborative-based selling to key clients.

Consultative selling helps to maintain margins through perceived and real demand for a customer's products. This is accomplished with an intimate understanding of the customer's business and category.

Consultative selling integrates nicely with negotiation planning in the following ways:

1)   Customers want creative ideas & solutions

Suppliers who offer ideas that either save the customer money or potentially grow sales will be invited to the negotiation party. A salesperson that consistently brings creative ideas/solutions to their customer's attention will be first in line.

With consultative selling, the salesperson who is thinking creatively and on-their-feet, understands and anticipates the customer's appetite for risk. As a result, these consultative salespeople will have greater access to direct customer conversations that convert into revenue opportunities.

It is important to note that our customers want to shine in front of their peers and their company superiors. If a customer has a germ of an idea and wants to collaborate with a key supplier in search of a finished solution, salespeople who are creative and consultative will be contacted more frequently.

2)   Customers and trust

Trust between two people is very personal. Consultative salespeople strive to hone and improve their trusted relationships with key customers. The importance of trust between a salesperson and the customer cannot be underestimated.

A former Director of Media Procurement for The Hudson's Bay Company once told me that trust was what separated the people who won deals with him versus those who didn't. He indicated that on a weekly basis, many proposals were forwarded to him, all with compelling offers and value equations. When it came down to choosing which deals to accept, he always asked himself which salespeople he trusted most. These were the salespeople who won the deals and are the people he relied on to execute professionally.

3)   Consultative salespeople move up the food chain

As a salesperson, if you are not in the first or second call position with your important customers, selling will likely be more expensive. Consultative salespeople understand that if they are in the third or lower call position that they will be forced to sell and negotiate at deeper prices. This means these third and lower position salespeople are at greater risk of having their products commoditized by the customer. It also forces these same salespeople to buy market share to stay at the table with important customers.

4)   Selling one of anything is just plain expensive

With the rising "cost of sale", why would sales management go to the expense of selling just one of anything to a customer?

Consultative selling encourages both buyers and sellers to look for more common ground because everyone benefits when both parties realize that a consultative sales relationship is based on trust, good value, collaboration, and a long-term view of the market.

An advanced proposition is to raise the bar in your sales organization with consultative selling integrated with business negotiations.

3

GOOD, BETTER, BEST NEGOTIATOR

As a life skill, business negotiation falls into a vague category. It's not really taught as a business skill until college or university. For the most part, it is not given the same importance as other business subjects such as math, accounting, finance, or marketing. Yet, in my conversations most business people profess to be good negotiators, even though they cannot describe a single negotiation strategy, philosophy, or process.

Many years in a successful business career have taught me that the subject of business negotiation is personal and even ego-driven. We spend a lifetime in business, bargaining and negotiating daily but ironically, we seldom take the time to read on the subject or better yet train to become proficient bargainers. Professional business negotiators live in the trenches and learn from the business titans in their respective business categories. Professional negotiators learn not from easy victories over weak adversaries, but by watching and making mistakes in large business negotiations. They learn by sweating for months over important or multi-million dollar deals that could possibly affect the job stability of their business colleagues. They also learn by running a post-mortem on every negotiation they complete grading it via a set of measurable benchmarks.

The reason I work so hard in business is for my family; I want to create a better life for them than I had growing up. So, why on earth would I allow myself to senselessly give away hard-earned cash in poorly executed business deals? Why wouldn't I try to be my best in negotiating deals, so my loved ones can enjoy a tiny bit more?

Here are five "life changing" reasons to become a better business negotiator:

1) **Business external** - If you're in business, you will likely engage with customers, suppliers, or both. When we negotiate business deals, you can expect that they will have a residual effect on future business. Our ability to negotiate smart, cooperative, profitable deals affords a sense of stability to our business world and to those we work with. The reason we work for smart cooperative deals is that we want the party we have negotiated with to complete their side of the agreement in good faith.

Cooperation in a negotiation has another affect: There are almost always problems that pop up with contract fulfillment. Smart, cooperative deals lay the groundwork for successfully working through smaller problems that must be negotiated to keep the contract delivery on track, on time, and on budget.

2) **Business internal** - I worked on the management team of Canada's largest newspaper company. We represented 125+ newspapers, and I can tell you without hesitation being a deft internal negotiator was critical. It seemed like every day was an internal negotiation marathon. The smartest professionals I worked beside became proficient at negotiating upward in the organization. They realized the greatest gains were achieved in bargaining with senior managers to get budget approvals, change policy, and making sure year-end bonuses got the full internal bargaining treatment. It pleases me when business leaders such as KPMG are preaching the concept of "low self-interest" to their employees and partners. If applied sincerely, low self-interest makes internal negotiations much more expeditious because it is built into the corporate culture.

3) **Large personal purchases** - The number of large personal purchases we make over a lifetime is mind boggling. We buy cars, homes, cottages, boats, vacations, financial services, home furnishings/renovations, and so on. It's not too long before this number reaches $1,000,000. Let me leave you with a simple

piece of negotiation arithmetic: Every single percentage point you can claim in a negotiation on $1,000,000 is worth $10,000.   Think of the possibilities.

4)   **Family negotiations** - Family negotiations are the most sensitive, especially when dealing with children and the elderly. Knowing how to prepare and present negotiations on delicate subjects is paramount. We always want everyone to feel like they're being heard and being fulfilled even under the most challenging of circumstances.   So the question is, can you gently weave negotiation skills into your family relationships for a better outcome?

5)   **Reputation** - Reputation is a variable in life affected on a 360 degree basis, in many cases without our knowledge. So, I take reputation in stride and let my positive actions speak loudest.   In a business negotiation setting, however, I want all those who know me or know of me to believe that I leave no stone unturned. I want them to believe they better have their game on if they plan to engage me.   Business negotiation is like entering a high-stakes poker game. Your   reputation and table presence matters. Real money is in play and points can be saved.

4

CREATE A PHILOSOPHY

When you ask most business people to describe how they negotiate, more times than not you get:

a)   A blank stare

b)   A blushed face

c)   A description of a three part process:

i.   There's a beginning

ii.   There's a middle

iii.   There's an end where we hopefully get a deal done

Professional negotiators just savor the opportunity to meet business people who have a limited view of business negotiations.   They love it when they are able to knock the other side back on their heels with a few finely crafted questions. Or, get the other side to feel uncomfortable with their position in the negotiation.

Patrick Tinney

When you think about all of the advances the modern business community has made in manufacturing, transportation, marketing, sales, accounting, database management, safety, risk management, and customer relationships you would have to think the same gains would be evident in business negotiation as it relates to philosophy and process.   Not so. It's baffling.

To this author, owning a philosophy before heading into any business negotiation is imperative. A negotiation philosophy in this context is a hierarchical view of bargaining. Philosophy helps guide and ground us.   It's an anchor in rough seas. It's a compass when we are confused and feeling a little lost. If you think about it, our business negotiation philosophy helps us answer difficult questions by its very existence.

1)   What is our taste for financial exposure?

2)   How do we feel about positive and negative risk?

3)   Where do customer relationships fit in?

4)   What do our business promises mean?

5)   How do we know when we have struck a profitable deal that will last?

Is there a one-size-fits-all philosophy for business negotiation? Not yet.   The reason is that societal norms, technology, markets, communication, and even civility change over time.   Business negotiation has a great deal of soft skills woven into its fabric. This brings out discussions around trust, honesty, and integrity. If you don't have an overarching business negotiation strategy, work toward one.   It will save you time, money, and heartache.   And, a business negotiation philosophy will better prepare you for negotiation professionals that thrive on low-hanging fruit.

If we could employ school yard strategy to the business negotiation process, we could work with 1) Need 'em 2) Got 'em 3) Trade 'em. Unfortunately, in high stakes bargaining, that will definitely leave a mark.   What buyers have come to understand, especially in down or buyer's markets, is that they can change the polarity of business negotiation by just starting with price.   For sellers, this is not only challenging, it is dangerous.

14

Process in business negotiation trains us to look at the bigger picture of the customer's needs and wants. More importantly it requires the seller to get her question/query hat on and ask a lot of questions that require descriptive answers. The answer the buyer provides gives the seller a greater sense of their urgency to satisfy quality issues, timing issues, or price range issues. In other words, the right information will give the seller the ammunition she needs to start thinking furtively to create a unique solution for this unique customer.

The finite need for process in business negotiation is that it provides both buyer and seller with a road map. Reconnaissance, Objectives, Cost modeling, and a BATNA (Best Alternative to a Negotiated Agreement) are all key. This allows either side to spin their process model many different ways to look for enticing entry points into the Bargaining Continuum (AKA as a ZOPA or Zone of Potential Agreement).

If managed correctly, process is a discipline that brings out the best in negotiators. Process allows negotiators to explore collaborative solutions without fear of veering too far off plan.

Business negotiation philosophy and process are also the gateway to smart business deals that last. Think of Philosophy and Process as the foundation and bones of a strong house. Once in place, they give us the confidence to explore the boundaries of what is cutting edge today and the bargaining norm of tomorrow.

5

HOW EFFECTIVELY DOES YOUR SALES TEAM NEGOTIATE?

The reason I am so fascinated by skills surrounding sales negotiation is because there are no rules. No boundaries. No normal. No constant. There is just an opportunity to build a bridge toward fulfillment for two parties with mutual interests and contiguous needs. A sales negotiation is a meeting of minds that exposes business objectives, expectation gaps, and collaborative opportunity.

In modern business, there has been an attempt by the academic and business community to rationalize negotiation into a "four-legged stool" surrounding a discussion of cooperative negotiation concepts and philosophy. The terms we hear very often are Win/Win, Win/Lose, and so forth as a vehicle to rationalize the path to closure of smartly-crafted business deals.

Years of business experience has taught me that when quarterly and year-end bonuses are being paid to sales and procurement professionals to close smart, profitable deals, the spectrum of opportunities means something different to everyone around the bargaining table.

With this in mind, we now explore the *Unlocking Yes* "five-legged stool" of business negotiation philosophy:

1)   **Win/Win** - Also known as "Cooperative Bargaining," this philosophy hinges on both parties searching for and finding mutual value.   Negotiation partners expand opportunities to find a path to positive closure of business negotiations concluding with a resounding "Yes."

2)   **Win/Lose** - Also known as "Game Theory Bargaining," this philosophy is based on the concept that at the conclusion of a game, we end up with a winner and a loser. In this scenario, the intended Winner will use all the tactics and strategies she/he can to win the game. "Yes" in this case means, "Yes.   I've won."

3)   **Lose/Win** - This negotiation concept could be seen as strategic negotiation.   As a business, we may be willing to actually lose money on a deal today so we can make money in the future.   In buyer's markets, sellers may use this strategy to lock up much needed market share in the hopes of weathering a longer range storm.

4)   **Lose/Lose** - I refer to Lose/Lose as a spoiler position. Meaning, if I can't win, then neither of us will win.   You might think this approach is a little small-minded but, believe me, it happens in business more than you might expect. Think of this technique as a blocker approach to a threatening business competitor.

5)   **Win a little extra** - This negotiation approach, known as "a bigger piece of the pie," suggests winning a little more in a negotiation entails creativity and determination while maintaining a solid client relationship.

By shear nature, the most influential countries in the world are built on entrepreneurial aspiration and competition.   Think countries such as Japan, China, South Korea, United States, Germany, Great Britain, Australia, and Canada, to mention a few.   From a business standpoint, some of these countries have business strategy and game theory built right into their cultural fabric.   Tony Fang, author of *Chinese Business Negotiation Style*, believes that negotiation stratagems driven by *The Art of War* by Sun Tzu are deeply embedded in most far eastern cultures   including China, Japan, and South Korea.   The net/net is that Chinese business negotiators start every negotiation believing they are going to win.

Patrick Tinney

According to Statistics Canada, the average Canadian household earns just under $3,000,000 over the course of 40 years. If this is the case, every single percentage point we can earn in a lifetime of negotiations for our families is worth about $30,000. This is a significant amount of money. The interesting thing about business is there are no barriers as to how much money we can make or save in business negotiations. Can you imagine the arithmetic at play when you start applying just a single percentage point to large corporations? The greater opportunity lies in the fact that the gains can be much larger than a single percentage point. So, this begs the question, "how effectively does your sales team negotiate" for your company.

6

TEN WINNING SALES NEGOTIATOR TRAITS

The very best sales negotiators are different beings; they exhibit a unique set of qualities and tendencies many of us just do not have within us. Some of the most wonderful negotiators I have ever had the pleasure to observe manage their adversaries like they were playing a casual game of Saturday night cards or a board game. Great negotiators are able to call on a deep well of IQ and EQ and rebalance both of these gifts at will. In my 30+ years in business the very best sales and business negotiators had learned, they were naturally gifted or mastered varying combinations of the following traits.

1)   **Inquisitiveness** - By nature, people with inquisitive minds are able ask great open-ended questions and rapidly think ahead to the next level of open-ended questions before we have even answered the first query. They are mental data miners.   As a result, they quickly and concisely get to the root of the customer's needs, demands, and wants.

2)   **Strategy** - Strategic thinkers see a business negotiation as a battlefield. They quickly assess the other side's strengths and weaknesses. They devise routes of engagement with plans and back-up plans to lull us to sleep, confuse us, and

comfort us all while they are quietly closing routes of escape for their negotiation partners.

3)   **Analytic process** - Here we have the number crunchers and the masters of logic. They induce outcomes and plans for deductive closure. Analytic thinkers bring out the beauty in numbers and bring light to the shadows in chaos which can confuse us in complicated negotiations.

4)   **Emotional intelligence** - Rather than IQ, it's EQ. It's a talent that helps you understand those around you without them saying much. Those with higher EQ detect body language, eye contact, change in mood, and atmosphere. They sense the other side by reading the room.   They have real empathy.

5)   **Risk assessment** - This is really a combination of analytic thinking and emotional intelligence.   It's how we gain the most in a negotiation while inserting positive risk while still getting a deal done.   When masterfully done, we maintain a strong relationship with our business negotiation partner.

6)   **Mental agility** - This is truly a great gift as it allows us to change risk and tactical gears in a negotiation to adapt to the other side without being detected. Mental agility makes us appear to be underwhelmed by quick changes in direction from your negotiation partner.   It gives us the confidence to stay grounded in the present and get deals done.

7)   **Time awareness** - Those who have awareness of real time can pace a negotiation to their advantage. They know how to compress and decompress time.   To a degree, it's like being a mental traffic cop.

8)   **Detail orientation** - Those who are detail-oriented know how to plan for a mission to get to closure rapidly.   As an example their pre-negotiation cost modeling is so well-placed, they know precisely when to move to a close. They also know, taking control the wording in contracts has the potential to work to their advantage.   They neutralize the other side with their advance reconnaissance.

9)   **Storytellers** - Raconteurs set the stage for negotiations with their ability to weave opposing interests together.   They know how to prime the well.   They add in anecdotal references to help negotiation partners understand why certain measures are recommended.   Storytellers make us feel good and help both sides cross the finish line to a positive deal.

10)   **Killer instinct** - Those with killer instinct are not afraid to seize an opportunity in a negotiation that may not appear again. They know some moments of truth that close negotiations need extra little push. This instinct is also about knowing when the other side is weak. Negotiators with killer instinct know perseverance is just part of the negotiation process.

So here's a question to all sales managers out there. How does your sales team measure up with the above traits? And, how are you going to improve their skills? With training, the above skills can be learned.

7

FOUR POWERFUL WORDS

There is a strong argument that "Yes" is the most powerful word in sales negotiations. I would like to challenge this argument and introduce three other very powerful words. The reason we are introducing these three other words as "powerful" is that without them a business negotiation process is too binary - just too black and white. For those of us who have concluded many complex business negotiations, we know that as revenue or expenditures rise, so too do the complexities of negotiations.

Here are the four most important words in business negotiation:

1)   **Need** - If there is no need, there is a low likelihood that a negotiation will take place. Need is the basis for most engagements with a buyer. If need is low on the part of the buyer, the seller has to come up with a perceived need or a new entry point in the discussion. If the seller has a low need, the buyer will just have to hold tight and wait for the next seller with a need.

The only other two situations where we will negotiate with another party in business are when we fear the other party or we just happen to like them.

Negotiating with a party we fear is not preferred. These deals tend to be lopsided and can be tainted with insecurity and distrust. What if the party we fear changes the rules of the negotiation? Will this make the situation better or worse and for how long?

Occasionally, we will conclude a deal with someone we like. However, these deals tend to be short-term unless some kind of fulfillment for the parties appears. Or, some need eventually appears that will cement the negotiation into a longer relationship. Most long-term business deals are logically based on need.

2)   **Trust** - Positive business relationships and negotiations rely on trust. Our trust in a negotiation partner allows us to get deals done more quickly. Trust allows us to explore higher ground and more inventive solutions in a negotiation.

Trust between two negotiation partners really lays bare the promises that parties make and keep on an hourly, daily, and yearly basis. Trust allows us to sleep at night. Trust allows us to lower our guard, knowing the other side will not take unnecessary advantage of us while completing the details of a deal.

3)   **Yes** - This is a fabulous word. The only problem with it is that it has limited use. In closing a negotiation, it only really gets used once. "Yes…we accept the terms and conditions of the negotiation and deal. Where do we sign?" There is no need to keep saying yes.

Yes can be used in other ways, though. Savvy negotiators will use the word *yes* as a momentum-builder in a negotiation. As a negotiator, I would use the word yes to reaffirm my relationship with the other side. I would get the other side used to saying yes to many smaller supporting parts of the negotiation. So, when it comes time to say yes to the signing of the deal, it does not seem like an awkward, anxiety-provoking word. At that point, the final yes is just a continuance of small agreements that cleared the way for the final pithy issues and a "Yes…where do we sign?"

4)   **No** - The word *no* is a great tactical word. It helps shape negotiations. A polite *no* will help us buy time until we have all of the right information or concessions. We can actually say no to the other side dozens and dozens of times without offending anyone. Both sides in a business negotiation realize that the word *no* helps us shape boundaries in a negotiation until everyone gets comfortable and then *no* is no longer necessary or relevant.

Patrick Tinney

So when considering a business negotiation, don't forget the words *Need*, *Trust*, *Yes*, and *No*. They are very powerful when used for effect, leverage, and closure. To help you remember, I leave you with this quote:

"We need to trust you so we can sort out the yeses and noes."
– Patrick Tinney

8

SUPERCHARGE YOUR SALES NEGOTIATION

Anyone who has ever been involved with a multimillion sales negotiation knows it can be an arduous, drawn-out affair. Depending on the complexity of the negotiation and all of the items the client has on their objective list, these negotiations can take months to complete. In most cases, the sales person on the account carries the largest responsibility for making sure the negotiation process moves forward at a timely pace. The sheer girth of the data and client issues that have to be captured can take an inordinate amount of time. Add to this that every issue the client raises generally has a dollar value attached to it. Of course, while our side is doing its best to offer client-driven solutions, there will be pressure to propose company-driven solutions based on our forward planning.

The theme of this approach is a logical plan. All we have to do is get a few of our smart people into a room and whammy....negotiation preparation problems become solved on our side. In theory, this should work. In practice, it can actually frustrate everyone including the customer, because the whole process actually slows down.

Patrick Tinney

What we really want to do is supercharge our business negotiation teams. Throughout my career, I have been involved in some really complicated client negotiations, requiring crack negotiation teams. Here are some of the things our teams did to reduce negative risk and raise our chances to consume a larger piece of the negotiation pie:

1)   **Admit your strengths** - Marcus Buckingham wrote a great book, *About Our Strengths.* He successfully argues that too often we in Western and Japanese corporate culture spend too much time focusing on our weaknesses. Therefore, if we are in a multimillion dollar pressure cooker, it is just plain smart to say in a team setting, *"This is what I am really good at. So, give me the following items to close out quickly, with the smartest solutions on hand."* Convince the others in your group to admit their strengths, and break the work to be done into consumable pieces.

2)   **Choose the right leader** - Being a leader and doing the most work do not necessarily mean the same thing. We mentioned earlier that the salesperson generally picks up most of the work in a customer negotiation, and this is generally true. But, what if the thrust of our objectives and forward planning are based on research or analytics? What if it is based on a creative- or production-based process that the sales person just does not have deep expertise in? The right leader then becomes the person who can drive the negotiation team expeditiously, even if they do not directly appear in front of the client and are possibly hidden behind "firewalls" during the face-to-face client negotiations.

3)   **Set internal timelines** - The short lesson here is if your negotiation team is not on an assignment completion timetable; your team will inevitably misuse time and drift.

4)   **Encourage creative thinking** - While I worked with some incredibly creative negotiators over the years, one person is an absolute standout - Don Fisher my manager on the Retail Team at The Southam Newspaper Group. Don had the ability to offer macroeconomic insights into the retail industry while thinking bottom-up with creative client incentive plans. He mashed merchandising, sales, and accounting to create a superior negotiation formula with incredible regularity. Don would draw the best product, trend, and research ideas from those he worked with, and then quietly drew his charges into what I refer to as a "positive risk" zone. The client proposals that came out of the environment that Don created

were second to none. He would also work to release steam and conflict within the team. On more than one occasion, I can remember him saying, *"You know, I just love it when customers hit us over the head because when they stop it feels sooo good."*

5)   **Second set of eyes** - When there are millions of dollars on the line, the multitude of moving parts in a negotiation can create an unwieldy mass. Be smart, and add a second set of critical eyes into your negotiation team. I cannot tell you how much time and money this has saved me and businesses that I have represented over the years. The best person in this important role that I've worked with is Debra Rother, currently a senior manager in Canada's magazine industry. Debra possesses four great gifts. She is a Spartan editor. Debra can analyze a client proposal and simultaneously offer client and senior management recommendations with confidence. She asks tough questions. And, Debra has a solid moral compass. All of the above traits are those of a trusted advisor when the negotiation team is getting bogged down in a huge negotiation.

6)   **BATNA-RAMA** - Since none of us is smarter than all of us, why not have several BATNA (Best Alternative To A Negotiated Agreement) in reserve. When you have a smart business negotiation team giving their very best to a good cause, make sure they all have an opportunity to vote on and rank this team's ideas and proposals.

7)   **Expect the unexpected** - Just because we have put smart people to work on our negotiation objectives, it doesn't mean the other side has not done the same or even raised the bar. There is a lot of warm and fuzzy conversation about Win/Win in business negotiations. Let's be honest, and realize that both the client's procurement team and our sales negotiation team get yearly raises and bonuses based on meeting and exceeding company negotiation objectives. I am a great proponent of signing deals that last over time and maintaining great customer relationships. I am also a great believer in meeting and exceeding my negotiation objectives.

8)   **At the bargaining table** - There are literally dozens of business negotiation strategies available to us in a bargaining session. Having a sharp team presenting and negotiating only increases our strategy repertoire. This allows different team members to play different but complementary roles at the bargaining table.

Patrick Tinney

Question: How supercharged are your business negotiation teams?

PART II - EXPLORATION

9

HIGH VALUE QUESTIONS...INVALUABLE

Curiosity in negotiations saves money.   It's as simple as that.

The way we channel our negotiation curiosity is to ask High Value Questions. High value questions are those that cannot be answered with a "yes" or a "no."

Examples of high value questions on negotiation training are:

1)   When and why was negotiation training introduced to your team?

2)   What was the big difference in your team after negotiation training?

3)   What aspect of negotiation training will be the most valuable to you and your company?

4)   Who on your team needs negotiation training?

5)   How much revenue is your company hoping to capture with negotiation training?

The person who curiously enquired using the above high value questions would certainly have gained a lot of information on:

1)   Timing

2)   Corporate culture

3)   Response expectations

4)   Goals

5)   Personnel

6)   Budget information

High value questions sometimes called "open-ended" questions are essential to collecting the kind of information from the other side that allows us to avoid making assumptions and costly mistakes in negotiations.

To put this in context, if a sales negotiation were a military exercise; can you imagine leading a team on to the battle field without having asked piercing questions to build reconnaissance on the opposing side?   Not likely.

An astute negotiator will have a list of high value questions in her pocket before she enters every client negotiation meeting.   These questions will be ranked by importance of revenue or objectives.

If the high value questions are delivered in a non-threatening manner, as the other side starts to answer at length, four important things should happen:

1)   The person on our team asking the questions should then assume the role of interviewer and gently encourage the other side to continue with their line of response so the interviewer can ask deeper questions.

2)   If our side is on a four-legged call with the client, the person not asking questions should be taking detailed notes.

3)   After the meeting, these notes are then dissected and matched against our ranked list of high value questions and objectives.

4)   Finally, a new set of high value questions is created for the next meeting in the negotiation.

The outcome of the meeting may not be as important as the information gathered through well-conceived high value questions.

High value questions in negotiations – invaluable.

10

"US & THEM"...TEN IMPORTANT QUESTIONS

Professional business negotiators make getting a smart deal look almost natural. When we watch them in action, we think they must have an innate talent for such transactions.

The reality is that good business negotiators are always working a plan that allows them to make intelligent decisions while the other side is still collecting or digesting information. If a good negotiator has collected the correct information, they will know when to say *yes* to maximize their yield.

Seasoned business negotiators start out by collecting data on their negotiations before the other side even realizes the game is on. They do this by asking questions that will help them shape their bargaining positions well in advance and save the final hours of the negotiations for revisions on plans. They do this while focusing on the other sides "tells" (bargaining signals) and emotional responses to needs and deadlines.

Good negotiators take as much negative risk out of negotiating as possible. They focus on enhancing positive risk and pulling the other side closer to their "comfort zone" in closing a good and wise deal. They do this while still maintaining a solid relationship with "Them" to get the deal done.

Below are 10 Important Question for "Us" to ask ourselves before we begin any negotiation. If you cannot answer the majority of the questions below with confidence, slow the negotiation down. You are moving too quickly. Ultimately, not knowing enough about "Them" will cost you money in the present and opportunities in the future.

10 Important Questions in a Negotiation:

1) Who understands risk better associated with the negotiation – us or the other side?

2) Who has the best intelligence on the negotiation – us or the other side?

3) Do we have their trust?

4) Do we understand their negotiation weaknesses?

5) Do we truly understand their needs?

6) Do we understand their objectives?

7) Can we empathize with their stance in the negotiation?

8) Do we understand their price/cost thresholds?

9) Do we have a proposal meaningful enough to them?

10) Do we feel confident enough to say yes to a good deal?

If you can confidently answer the majority of our top 10 then you are ready to move forward. Be patient and persevere. Most large negotiations do not conclude on the first pass. Close the deal if it is smart and profitable.

One more important thing: make sure our team writes the contract. There will always be points in a negotiation that require further definition. We want to craft the document associated with these bargaining points in our language.

Finally, congratulate yourself. You did it. There is always learning in every negotiation. No two negotiations are identical. What did you learn from "them" this time that will improve your position for next time?

11

PROFIT THROUGH DISCIPLINED LISTENING

In big money sales negotiations, we have to train ourselves to become professional listeners or risk losing out on millions of dollars in sales, savings, or future opportunities.

By nature, most of us are not great listeners. Many sales and procurement professionals distract easily. Technology including cell phones, smart phones, and other omnipresent hand-held devices only exacerbates our inability to concentrate. I once had a boss who used to have a television blaring in his office quite often and confessed to having the attention span of a nat.

The difference between business negotiations and other business functions is that you really only get one shot at getting it right. In other words, when you have completed a negotiation, the last thing you want to do is to re-open the negotiation and risk losing what you have gained in the first pass.

To improve your listening skills in big negotiations, I recommend:

1)   **Planned meeting objectives** - Do not enter into a negotiation hoping to think on your feet or depend on your ability as a counter puncher. If we have well-planned meeting objectives for each bargaining session, we will have already thought through our strengths, weakness, opportunities, and threats as well as those of our bargaining partner. This information is helpful in creating our business negotiation tactics and strategy. It will lead to a line of persuasive thinking that will help draw the other side closer to our objectives. It also helps us to listen for certain pieces of information to verify or denounce our knowledge base and strategy.

2)   **Ranked high value questions** - In sales negotiations high value questions are money questions. Questions, that begin with who, why, where, when, what, how or which. They encourage descriptive answers. I call them money questions because I want to rank questions in terms of importance to the negotiation.   The questions with the greatest importance to a negotiation generally have the highest correlation to the revenue/budget. For example, "who in your organization will benefit most from our proposal?" Listening carefully to the answers to these money questions allows our side to ask even deeper questions. It also opens up even greater chances for deeper listening if we can discipline ourselves to remain silent while the other side responds.

3)   **No unnecessary technology** - If you are going to engage a client and can do so without the use of a smart phone, turn it off. How can you listen if you are glancing at a smart phone while your bargaining partner is answering money questions? Don't let technology cost you a profitable opportunity regarding money questions. Remember if your bargaining partner slips and gives you a sensitive piece of information, it is doubtful they will repeat it.

4)   **Stay in the present** - Focus your thought process so you do not drift backward and forward too much when you are listening to the other side answering high value questions.   By keeping your mind anchored in the precious present you will hear more, and you will notice more of their body language.   This will help you make better decisions about their bargaining position.

5)   **Using a note taker** - I cannot tell you how advantageous it is to have a note taker in a business negotiation.   This creates an opportunity for one person to ask high value questions and listen, totally focused on our negotiation partner's response.   It allows the person asking the questions to have a great impact on the

speed and tempo of the negotiation session. It may mean our side will get more of our money questions answered. The note taker focuses all their energy on capturing the maximum amount of information for later review.

6)   **Practice** - It's tough to listen when you have great ideas or quick fixes for problems competing for dominance in your mind. Silence is golden in a business negotiation. Especially, after you've asked the high value, money question that has the potential to be the tipping point in a big business negotiation.

If you are not a great listener, admit it to yourself and practice more. Disciplined listening does lead to greater business negotiation profits.

12

TRUE GENIUS IN RECONNAISSANCE

Winston Churchill was one of the finest strategists and negotiators in modern history

What Mr. Churchill clearly understood, and made great strides to improve, was knowledge about all influential political entities around him. He wanted to understand the strength and reliability of his Second World War allies such as France, Canada, USA, et al. More importantly, he had to gather "reconnaissance" (recon) on his enemies and potential invaders of the United Kingdom.

Recon in business negotiation has just as vital a role.

Owing to time compression, budgetary pressures and anxiety, too often business negotiation partners will pull chairs up to the bargaining table without enough recon on the other side. Not only does this affect your BATNA (Best Alternative Next Agreement), it can also have an effect on your team's confidence in staking a position in the "Bargaining Continuum" (AKA ZOPA or Zone Of Potential Agreement).

The reason we try to uncover as much information in "recon" is to improve the chances of neutralizing the other side who may believe they have unique information that will influence the outcome of the negotiation in their favor. By neutralizing the other side, they will not "run the table with momentum" and push us back on our heels, forcing us to catch up on business intelligence.

There is limitless information we can gather on our business negotiation partners however, recon genius can be found in the following five topics:

1)   **Shared business economics** - Knowing the economic futures and pressure points of our business compared to that of our negotiation partner will reveal potential strengths or weaknesses.

2)   **New business issues or opportunities** - Understanding new business issues or opportunities for both negotiation partners will help us frame our objectives as well as business concessions we will want to table during bargaining.

Understanding our partner's objectives will also give us a clearer sense of how far apart we are on key revenue issues. Topics may include new product introductions, new location launches, expansion or business contraction planning, and finally, rate increases.

3)   **Points of difference (POD) for both** - Having a clear understanding of our and their POD will give us the confidence to state our rationale for our costs and pricing. POD also speaks to uniqueness, scarcity, and demand for our product as well.

4)   **Cost offsets for both** - Arriving at any negotiation understanding in ranked order what you can afford to offer the other side without crippling your own business negotiation objectives is paramount.

Cost offsets do not necessarily mean money. It could be access to technology, relaxed timelines for delivery/warehousing of product, or for payment schedules. It could also mean access to new services your company is about to offer. Services that the rest of the market place has not yet seen, but, they could help your negotiation partner improve their market position. Understanding cost offsets is creatively using what you may have already developed at little cost or absorbed as a cost that can now be passed along as a bargaining chip. Don't always start with money.

5)   **Profile of negotiators** - Often in large business negotiations, we do a lot of ground work and preparation with one business contact only to find out that a different person will be the lead negotiator for our partners at the bargaining table. If you find out that your partner is moving in a new associate to head their negotiations, make sure you find out all you can about the new person's ethics, reputation, likes, dislikes, values, and affiliations. All of this information will help you build a profile on this person and improve your ability to soften the impact of the new negotiator for their team.

Finally, work at incorporating "true genius" into your business negotiations with crafty recon. Remember Winston Churchill and how he shaped his surroundings by having the capacity for evaluation of uncertain, hazardous, and conflicting information.

13

BRAND ALIGNMENT AND ITS INFLUENCES IN A SALES NEGOTIATION

Brand Alignment in the contemporary sense, is the alignment of all communication, cultural, and marketing efforts. This presents a brand as one continuous stream of thought to the consumer.

Alternatively, we want to present brand alignment as an alignment of corporate position in the market, relative to your clients and your selling peers. In sales negotiation, brand alignment has the potential to greatly influence your BATNA.

Brand alignment for corporate negotiation partners could mean you have customers, standards of excellence, or aspirations in common. These common elements naturally create an attraction for doing business together. Therefore, negotiating with a business partner whose needs profile fits your own makes for a matching or more-leveled playing field. For example, in a previous life, I worked in the daily newspaper business. One of the closest matches we had from a customer market profile perspective was the major department stores. Research at the time pointed out that our daily newspaper readers were also very much aligned to the major department store customer ideal. This did not mean our business negotiations were "open net goals". It only meant we both understood we had a lot of common ground that was compelling.

This alignment can happen anywhere in the business spectrum from the ultra-high end of the business market to the low end of the business market. The cliché *"birds of a feather flock together"* comes to mind.

So, if direct brand alignment is a benefit to both parties in a business negotiation, what does it mean for businesses that are interested in each other but are further up or down the ideal pecking order? In a word, it's a "challenge."

In Toronto, Canada, we are blessed with six daily newspapers. To one degree or another all of these newspapers are either very well aligned to specific readers and advertisers, or they are in a ranked pecking order up or down. In this setting, residing in the first or second market preference position with an advertiser is a much sought after negotiation position. Residing in the third or fourth market preference positions becomes a negotiation challenge. Those daily newspapers on the perimeter high or low market positions have a huge challenge convincing advertisers that they are simpatico with opposite brand customers and quality requirements.

We have used daily newspapers as an example but, the same conversation about brand alignment in business negotiation could just as easily been shifted to home appliances, tablet computing devices, or packaged goods.

Elements that equalize a lack of brand alignment at the bargaining table include creativity, innovation, quality, technology, timing, and price:

Creativity - Customers buy creative ideas over stuff any day of the week. Your company may be in the number three pecking position but if you have creative solutions for a customer that attract new markets and add value, this is a great brand alignment equalizer.

Innovation - This is where we take unique brand parts and do something really neat to help our customer be smarter, faster, or better. If you can show a customer how to make money, you are bound to get a longer client engagement. Innovation is an equalizer.

Quality - Having access to various iterations of your product in various sizes, styles, positions, formats, or color is an attention-grabber. If your company has the ability and agility to modify quality of a product to suit a budget or a market place, you are showing great flexibility. Guess what? We have another brand alignment equalizer.

Technology - Lots of customers love to be on the cutting edge of technology to give them an advantage in the market over their competitors. Technology may be something your company owns and has already paid for. It could be a new use of the Internet. It could be as simple as a new use for a symbol. Just think a few years ago, hardly anyone had heard of a *"Quick Response Code"*. For those who first adopted QR codes they had a period of stylish, nerdy, uniqueness so sought after in today's fickle consumer and business market.

Timing - Finding or saving time has the potential to give customers a strategic advantage over competitors and quite possibly save them money in the process. Another great brand alignment equalizer.

Price - We've purposely saved price until last because anyone can lower price without thinking about the long-term ramifications this causes their brand. And, the very alignment they are seeking with a potentially important customer.

If we are lowering price for a well-placed strategy - bravo! If we are lowering price to maintain market share and keep feeding the troops – brave, but what is your exit plan? If we are buying business to make it to the next round of payments, then I say, over to you.

When your company is trying to solve the problem of brand alignment in business negotiations make sure your team does a customer needs assessment first. Think creativity, innovation, quality, technology, and timing to level the playing field. Leave price last.

14

DEFINE OBJECTIVES. NEGOTIATE LIKE A PRO

Throughout our lives we are coached by parents, teachers, and business leaders to "plan our work and work our plan". The "plan our work" part means we should be wise with our time, implement our skills to their highest and best use to achieve goals.

Sound easy?

One would think as we get ready to head into a negotiation of any kind that the first thing we would do is to sit down and plan our work with objectives that are measurable, quantitative, and qualitative.

It would also stand to reason that if we are going to negotiate with a partner and sell/present our position, we would take the time to clearly think "their position" through. This will allow us to have all possible counter arguments researched and in place to help us achieve the best outcome for our side.

Make sense?

Surprisingly, a large percentage of the time, private citizens and business professionals walk into negotiations with little more than their "wish list" for a positive outcome.

In other words, we push our stuff up on to the table for "them" to see and try to convince the other side that they should comply with our needs, or else.

Visualize us walking into an automobile dealership and telling them we need a car. We need their best deal. We want a discount. Then we ask them what deals they've got.

Oh, Oh.

This is just about the time "we" get creamed. We start back-peddling as we try to digest a barrage of unanticipated data, information, figures, and defensive emotion from the other side.

As it turns out, they were better prepared than we were and actually sold us on their needs. And we ended up buying into a scenario we had not counted on.

How did this happen?

Let's go back to the beginning of "planning our work and working our plan". It's cliché but astute. Those who take the time to:

1)   List their objectives in ranked order of importance

2)   Attach a dollar figure to each objective

3)   Do the above for the other side

4)   Imagine and list "their" arguments

5)   Think about and understand "their" needs

6)   Have empathy for "them"

7)   Understand the expectation gap between "us and them"

8)   Position us to persuasively pull "them" toward us

9)   And, negotiate a wise and profitable deal that fulfills both "us and them"

This is how pros make concluding deals look so easy. They take the time to learn as much as possible about the other side. Pros rank, quantify, and match their needs and objectives with those of their partners. Pros measure risk, have empathy, build plans, and positively plan their work to completion.

Top pros even sit down after a successful deal has been completed to try to pinpoint their own shortcomings for improvement next time. The best negotiators are students who always learn from the other side.

Negotiate like a Pro.

15

CASH IS KING...THE BUYER'S MARKET

"Cash is King." If you weren't familiar with this phrase, you are now.

During any national or international economic upheaval, it will change the way we all negotiate. Lenders are skittish. Budgets are scrutinized for efficiencies. Uncertainty will be upon us. Organizations and individuals with cash are in a position to call the shots for a period of time.

For buyers of a variety of products and services, this means you have a much wider assortment of buying strategies at your disposal. You are in the enviable position to say no to as many offers as you choose because sellers are lining up to see you.

Buyers, your IQ will appear to have risen exponentially because sellers will be listening to and dissecting every word you say looking for signs of a *maybe* or a *yes*.

Buyers, this is your time. You can compress time. You can elongate time. You are actually in good position to bend time and turn time back on pricing.

Sellers, the world just got little more complicated. The marketplace will be taking more time to make decisions about your needs. If your offerings are not absolutely unique and compelling, you will be pressed to show substantially more value than in the past just to maintain market share. This will require you to be the best negotiator at the table or face declining profit.

Seller negotiation strategies that worked last week may not be relevant this week. Relationships with buyers will change because the market is now wired differently. Even those sellers who are market leaders with great value propositions and dominant points of difference will be doing their utmost to lock up as much available revenue from buyers as possible. Why? Because "Cash is King".

Once a dominant seller has secured enough market share and revenue to keep their bankers and shareholders at bay, these sellers will become comfortable projecting forward, and, only then be in a position to negotiate tougher deals.

For us in business who are not selling a monopoly, we can only "walk away" from a piece of business if it is damaging to us or if we have an equal or better opportunity elsewhere. Dominant sellers that lock up base revenue with smart negotiations will have more confidence to negotiate future peripheral or pedestrian deals.

There may even be sellers who are going to be placed in positions where they may actually be forced to buy business in some negotiations. It sounds odd, but it's true.

Now, because "cash is king," buyers will feel strong enough to start contacting sellers and asking them "would you take this offer?" A buyer's market is wired differently; transactional roles may actually be reversed. Seller negotiating skills will truly be tested.

In this environment sellers will have to:

1)   Truly understand the negotiating process

2)   Have better reconnaissance than the other side

3)   Understand our SWOT (strengths, weaknesses, opportunities, and threats) and that of the other side

4)   Make objectives clear and ranked for importance

5)   Have deep empathy for the other side

6)   Cost model propositions, so as agreements close, they support our objectives

7)   Be flexible with negotiations that show unusual elasticity

8)   Make proposals relevant to buyers. Buyers with cash seek "unique propositions"

9)   Know their operations so deeply they can say "yes" confidently

10)   Be brave. Be strong. Build Smart/Wise Deals

Remember "cash is king".

16

POWER SWOT BEFORE MAJOR SALES NEGOTIATIONS

A very powerful exercise prior to any major sales negotiation is a SWOT (strengths, weaknesses, opportunities, and threats) analysis of our business relative to the negotiation. Professional sales negotiators may go much further with this exercise and SWOT their competitors and their bargaining partner.

Why SWOT? The answer is why wouldn't you? This analysis, if performed honestly, helps us bring greater light to our position with our bargaining partner. It also helps us formulate strategy, plans, and tactics that we may want to bring to the negotiation table.

The SWOT exercise sounds pretty academic, but it's surely the one that gives sales people the greatest uneasiness. While training a very mature sales force, I was amazed that SWOT analysis of a negotiation was an "AHA Moment" for them.

It can be difficult for us to be objective, especially when facing a potentially difficult business negotiation. Most of us also have a fairly easy time discussing our strengths and opportunities, because as business people, we live in the present and future where we are strong and robust. We sell and negotiate best when we project from a position of strength.

Also, in corporate life, it's not very popular to speak excessively about weaknesses and threats. After all, aren't we professionals at turning customer objections into sales? Can't we just figure this problem out and come up with a sensible solution?

By honestly detailing weakness and threats, we are opening the door to intelligent discussion about business implications. This can actually help us raise our game, fix holes in our defense and be better prepared to hear customer objections. By showing empathy, this allows us to honestly say, "We, too, are concerned about this issue, and this is what we are doing to address this weakness." Honesty has the potential to hasten strategic solutions and possibly thwart competitors with our innovative ideas.

Back to the positive: By studiously adding up our strengths and opportunities, we can clearly see key leverage points we can use to persuade our bargaining partners to move closer to our negotiation objectives. After all, doesn't everyone want to participate with a winner, especially, if both sides in a negotiation experience financial and emotional fulfillment?

What about a SWOT analysis on our closest competitors? Smart move. My lifetime in business has taught me there are simply no safe accounts, no safe markets, and no safe deals. Our competitors are constantly changing the playing field with new innovations, new product launches, new acquisitions, and new partnerships.

For example, in recent years we see suppliers move their own people into customers head offices and become a seamless, influential part of the customer's team. The rub is that these suppliers are doing this by assuming the cost of equipment and personnel to take pressure of diminishing resources on the customer's side. The upside is that these suppliers are solidifying long-term deals with this strategy.

Finally, what about a SWOT analysis of our bargaining partner? Doubly smart move. This focuses us on understanding their world with greater intensity and empathy. If they are trying to build revenue or market share that we can positively affect through our innovation – what a gift of knowledge this is heading into a negotiation.

On the other hand, by understanding their weaknesses and threats we can ask some pretty well-placed questions about what is keeping our negotiation partner up at night. Again, all of this information just strengthens our ability to be more decisive with our negotiation strategy.

By trying to see ourselves through our customer's eyes we are really exposing our side to the deepest truth one can hope to uncover prior to a negotiation. What if we are in love with our "point of difference" in the market, but our customer could really care less and actually does not agree with our wonderful assessment of us? Yikes!

The neat thing about all of the above analysis is that if time is compressed, you can actually write a mini SWOT on the back of a napkin sitting in a waiting room heading into a negotiation meeting. This advanced negotiation technique is how negotiation professionals scratch out those precious, extra points at the negotiation table.

So here's the question: How good and dedicated is your team at SWOT analysis, heading into major negotiations? If the answer is "not great," I highly recommend you seek out a professional negotiation facilitator to help your team learn to Power SWOT effectively to scratch out those precious, extra points at the negotiation table.

17

SWOT COMPETITORS BEFORE NEGOTIATIONS

Preparation for major sales negotiation involving million dollar contracts takes a wider swath. Not only do you need to have a great proposal in hand with creative BATNA options, you need to be prepared for a feisty battle with competitors who are trying to expand their position with your customer.

A thorough SWOT of your competitor's position in your industry often yields great ideas for your upcoming key customer negotiations. By looking at our competitor's strengths/opportunities and weaknesses/threats, we will identify the gaps between our offerings and other important information. This will help us gain the upper-hand and grow our share of business with major customers.

To begin, we must gather every piece of available information on our competitor through industry analysis, quarterly stock market reports, business blogs/articles, and of course our competitor's website. This sounds like a huge undertaking but, with robust search engine capabilities and crafty queries, you'd be surprised what you can gather with a few stealthy clicks.

There is no perfect place to start a SWOT analysis, but I prefer to know as much about our competitor's strengths/opportunities also known as "Key Leverage Points." They will almost always base their proposals with key leverage points, highlighting their unique product and service offerings in the market place. I want to know these key leverage points before I stand in front of a frosty customer who may use my competitor's offerings as a tool to dampen or diminish our proposal.

Our competitors key leverage points (strengths/opportunities) may include:

1)   New product development

2)   New technology

3)   New markets

4)   Strategic alliances

5)   Cutting edge research

6)   Innovative test results

7)   Flexible packaging and delivery

8)   And….great pricing

By understanding competitor key leverage point data, I will be able to adjust our proposal to address the issues above that we believe are game-changers for our large customer. With this preparation, the customer will respect the amount of time we have taken to analyze and anticipate their key needs, so they are not under pressure to make unnecessary, stressful, supplier changes.

Next, I want to know all about our competitor's weaknesses/threats also known as "Business Implications." By understanding my competitor's daily worries (business implications), I can strategically weave this intelligence into our proposals to our major client and to our advantage.

Notable business implications (weakness/threats) we look for will include:

1)   Geographical gaps

2)   Technology glitches

3)   Misaligned market offerings

4)   Quality performance

5)   Supply chain bottlenecks

6)   Staffing/union problems

7)   Senior management stability

8)   Storage/delivery reliability and tracking

9)   Problem resolution response times….to mention a few...

When I am able to effectively bundle a 360 degree analysis of our competitors through a SWOT analysis, I am able to plan for most large customer queries during a negotiation. Our mission is to respond with quick, crisp competitor alternatives in a live bargaining setting. We follow up this action with objection handling value statements that could begin as follows:

"We hear what you are saying. We have been monitoring these events in the market. We appreciate your interest and concerns. Speaking of which, here is a great solution and opportunity we have developed. We look forward to sharing it with you and your team of experts for seamless implementation. This is why our customers continue to call us first because we develop creative solutions. We anticipate critical needs."

Be smart. Continue to expand your share of your customer's available expenditures. Power SWOT your competitors so you can focus more on the customer's needs while producing creative, revenue-winning proposals during complicated large account business negotiations.

18

SWOT YOUR CUSTOMER BEFORE A SALES NEGOTIATION

Performing a SWOT analysis on a major customer before a business negotiation is not only smart, it is a necessity. It is analogous to a surgeon taking an MRI x-ray of a patient before performing major surgery. If your customer negotiation is critical to your company, the depth of the SWOT analysis should reflect this.

When we combine the customer's strengths and opportunities (key leverage points), we are looking for openings to help the customer drive their business propelled by our products and services. If we can approach the customer negotiation with creative ideas helping to crystalize their opportunities that appear out of reach for them, all the better for our cause at the bargaining table. This allows us to table unique solutions for unique clients that are not as price-sensitive.

Let's face it: customers know they have pain points. I do believe the scale has tipped too far in many sales categories in driving this dogma home. "We've all been to the business house of horrors." Instead, let's talk to the customer about great beginnings and great untapped opportunities that only we can provide with our point of difference.

Our customer's key leverage points (strengths/opportunities) may include:

1) New product development

2) New technology or better supplier sourcing

3) New product launches

4) Unique points of difference

5) Unique product or market verticals

6) New markets

7) Strategic purchases causing potential new efficiencies

8) Faster and more flexible packaging and delivery

9) Traditional and 2.0 Sales Possibilities plus great pricing

With this preparation, the customer will respect the amount of time we have taken to analyze and anticipate their key needs. This type of positive risk thinking on our part is a "game-changer."

Next, I want to know all about our customer's weaknesses/threats, also known as "Business Implications." By understanding my customer's daily worries (business implications), I can strategically weave this intelligence into our proposal, again, to our advantage.

Notable business implications (weakness/threats) we look for will include:

1) Market share erosion

2) Profit erosion

3) Geographical gaps

4) Technology shortcomings

5) Traditional customer competitors

6) Non-traditional customer competitors

7)   Over supply positions

8)   Recent internal and external sales disruptions

9)   Brand instability/erosion

When I am able to effectively bundle a 360 degree analysis of our large customer through a SWOT analysis, I am able to think as if I were walking in their shoes. We want our proposal to be meaningful, constructive, and incremental to their business. If we get the trajectory of our proposal right and presented to key decision makers, it opens up the possibility for a stream of trial closes that might sound like this:

a)   *"What about our proposal did you like the most?"*

b)   *"Who in your organization will benefit from our proposal?"*

c)   *"How would you like to begin rolling out our proposal?"*

Winning in a large customer business negotiation starts by thinking like an insider. If we can figure out where the customer sees the greatest opportunity for growth or the greatest need for defensive measures, then we are part of their team. Think in terms of the customer's culture and forward strategic planning. Breathe their rarified air, and you will be rewarded for your extra effort.

PART III - Relationships & Trust

19

BUILDING TRUST

Trust enters into so many facets of sales negotiation that, at times, it can make your brain hurt. Trust is the heart of most negotiations; if you don't trust the parties you are negotiating with, chances are, you will take extra steps to limit your risk exposure. These extra risk insurance steps can actually get in the way of exposing great mutual negotiation opportunities.

Conversely, if we are open to trusting the party we are negotiating with, the possibility of collaboration gets brighter. Both parties may actually positively nudge each other to take greater positive risk in cementing new accretive agreements that benefit both parties.

While working for a National magazine, I found myself in the middle of an $800,000 sales negotiation where I asked my Sales Director, David Titcombe to trust me at the same moment I was asking an important customer to trust me. Talk about a pressure cooker.

I had just presented what I thought was a very strong proposal to secure the $800K with lots of value added and great guaranteed advertising positions in the magazine becoming of a marquee advertiser. Our customer carefully looked over our proposal. There was a thoughtful, short pause, and the lead negotiator for the customer team looked over at us and told us our offering was "just not good enough." I listened to the customer and reaffirmed her concern and then did something that gave my Sales Director "The Willies." I asked the team for a time out. I wanted to think about our proposal and discuss options privately with my boss. My gut told me we were close, and I really wanted this deal.

The customer smiled and agreed to the short break. As we walked out of the room, David looked me in the eyes and said, "Tinney, I hope you know what you are doing." The funny part of this story is that I had called for a time out in the heat of the moment but had forgotten that we were in the customer's building and we had nowhere to go. We found a quiet corner and discussed ou options/BATNA. There is also a catch. When you are the one who calls for a break at an impasse in a negotiation, you must return to the negotiation table with a new and more valuable offer to the other side. Otherwise, you look arrogant and, in a word, dumb. This is a trust killer.

We returned to the bargaining table with a few new ideas to enhance our proposal. We got the deal done. We all got what we wanted. Everyone trusted; everyone won.

Below are five tips to build trust in business negotiations. Remember, trusted people get more deals done:

1)   **Listen to them** - If you want to build trust with a negotiation partner, you have to treat them as a unique person. Everyone has objectives, goals, and aspirations. We have angst. We all have a story. We have worries and bills to pay. And, most importantly, we have loved ones to care for. If we thoughtfully listen to our negotiation partners and ask the right questions, they will take notice. They will trust you more and more often.

2)   **Succeed with deeds** - Trust doesn't just happen. Someone has to start to build a foundation of trust. Someone has to take a positive risk and initiate the trust process. Take the leap of faith. Be the negotiation partner who says, "Here is something we value that I know will enhance our negotiation discussions."

3)   **Creative solutions** - Sharing creative ideas is definitely a way to build trust.   Customers buy ideas; they only buy stuff when they have no other choice. What new ideas are you bringing to your next negotiation?

4)   **Offer value** - In a Seller's Market we used to say, "Build it and they will come."   The problem with this thinking is that we have been in a Buyer's Market for many years, and those who are buying want two dollars of value for every dollar they spend.   This puts extra pressure on our point of difference and our value equation.   If you offer true value, they will trust you more.

5)   **Show up** - We trust personal brands not corporate brands in business negotiations.   This means that we trust people, not company names and titles.   It also means our personal brand is really a summation of our reliable, repeatable promises.   When I engage business partners with Centroid Training and Marketing, I ask them one simple question, "Will you show up?"   If there is the slightest bit of hesitation in my business partner's reply, I will ask for an explanation.

Trust is owed to no one.   Trust is earned.   Trust cannot be expected. Trust is given in good faith.   How do you build trust in important business negotiations?

20

RELATIONSHIPS MATTER

A group of buyers I trained a while ago asked me the following questions:

Are relationships really needed, or should I be harsher in business negotiations? Am I exposed if I have a relationship with a negotiation partner?

These queries underline the pressure and tumult buyers face in the uncertainty of our current economic conditions. Buyers start to second guess their core business beliefs and values in an effort to excel at the bargaining table.

As long as buyers are respectful and have a degree of empathy for their seller negotiation partners, acting firmly or weak is just part of the dance. Compressing or decompressing time is just an everyday tactic used in a negotiation.

There are dozens of tactics and strategies that professional buyers use in negotiations to unbalance the seller. The buyer's job is to move the seller off their script quickly so the buyer can start asking armor-piercing questions that the seller may not have prepared for. This helps pull the seller closer to the buyer's negotiation objectives.

We must not, however, leave our bargaining partners unfulfilled by a negotiation. Sellers that feel like they have been "taken to the cleaners" may start to resent a negotiated deal. Once resentment sets in, the deal will start leaking oil. Problems that inevitably pop up may not be handled well, placing the contract fulfillment at risk.

Solving problems is just part of business life. However, solving a problem for someone with whom we have a positive, trusting relationship will get greater attention. It's more than just a problem; it is a creative process to try and help a friend in need.

At the end of a multi-million dollar contract negotiation with one of Canada's largest department stores, I made a mistake in a very quick verbal exchange with a buyer. It was an honest misunderstanding. It meant our side would end up banking hundreds of thousands of incentive dollars that my buyer would not know about until we were very deep into the contract.

I was really happy to have signed the contract ending a long multi-million dollar negotiation, but as I started to recount the mistaken exchange on the way back to the office, I knew I had a huge problem. Approaching my sales manager at the time, I explained the situation. He told me not to worry and just wait for time to expose the problem, and we'd deal with it then.

This didn't sit right with me. I knew this was a career-defining moment. With my sales manager's reluctant blessing, I set up another meeting with my buyer. I exposed the mistake and extended apologies. The buyer quietly mulled the situation over for a minute, and he asked me to correct the mistake in the contract so he could sign it. He also told me my quick action clearly saved him a lot of budgeting grief later in the contract. Problem solved. End of story. Well, not quite.

Years later, our company changed ownership and was embroiled in a painful restructuring. Many jobs at my firm were lost in restructuring and there were stories in the news about more to come. My phone rang at the office. It was the same department store buyer mentioned above. He asked me how I was doing and was there any uncertainty around my future. He told me not to worry. He explained that he had already started making calls on my behalf and that if my job was lost, I would be working within days with his industry influence. Negotiation relationships matter.

As a buyer, I would rather have a negotiation relationship with the seller than not. My reasoning is simple: I am responsible for how much the other side knows about the inner workings of my company. In this, my exposure is measured and calculated.

My goal is to reduce negative risk and raise positive risk with information sharing. As partners, we move toward positive two- way communication. I do this to pull them closer to my buyer negotiation objectives. Ultimately, this will strengthen the relationship and raise the spectrum of getting a long-lasting, smart deal done.

Final thoughts: I recently polled some seller colleagues about being treated harshly or being commoditized at the negotiation table. Almost all sellers had a similar response which was, *"Do I take my best creative ideas to a buyer with whom I have a good relationship? Or do I turn to someone who thinks nothing of my company and has taken advantage of me?"*

The seller group was not filled with alacrity about the notion of sharing great ideas with negotiation users and abusers. Negotiation relationships do indeed matter.

21

E.Q. Versus I.Q. in Sales Negotiation

How important are E.Q. skills (soft, intuitive, people skills) vs. I.Q. skills (hard, process skills) in sales negotiation?

Edward de Bono gave us some clues with his creative thought mapping book, *Six Thinking Hats*. Edward argued successfully I believe that if we were able to categorize thought into White Hat (Straight Data) and Blue Hat (Straight Process), we could look at problems without emotion. He also argued that looking at problems or opportunities with Yellow Hat (Unbridled Enthusiasm) and Red Hat (Unfettered Emotion) could bring our gut feel and wonderful sense of alacrity to almost any situation. Red Hat can also bring in a sense of uneasiness as well. It is a raw emotive state. Finally, Edward gave us Green Hat (Unbridled Creativity) and Black Hat (Devil's Advocate) to balance both E.Q. and I.Q. into a single thought process.

Soft, intuitive skills in sales negotiation are largely overlooked or undervalued against the sexiness of cool terms like BATNA or ZOPA (Zone of Potential Agreement) by the academic crowd. How did we get deals done in the B.B.Z. days (Before BATNA and ZOPA)?

Did soft, intuitive skills play a more significant role B.B.Z.? Have we supplanted soft, intuitive skills with process that may be unbalancing our bargaining effectiveness? As a negotiator of multi-million dollar deals, I recognized that I used my soft, intuitive skills to gain information and pull negotiation partners closer to my objectives. I would do so by observing their language, body language, energy levels, emotional swings, deferral tactics, and anxiety levels. I also prided myself on the types of questions I asked and my listening skills. These are coupled with a great sense of empathy and compassion in order to get deals done.

Winston Churchill was a superlative negotiator. He knew how cut to the pith on complicated subjects and negotiations to bring them to life. We know he was a charismatic, master of reconnaissance and strategy. Strategy in itself contains a ranking of plans and backup plans. What skills did he use before BATNA and ZOPA? Is it possible he used softer, intuitive skills than we use today?

Back to Edward De Bono, you don't have to agree with the concept of *Six Thinking Hats*, but you have to admire him taking a stab at trying to create a new model from which to solve problems or capitalize on opportunities using E.Q and I.Q. transparently.

It's a little like training your mind to relax or ignore pain. It's just a style of thinking to lift us to a greater sense of awareness.

One of the undeniable elements of negotiation is momentum. Momentum leads toward tipping points. How do we gain momentum if the negotiation is just process? You could argue that if our BATNA is better than our bargaining partners, we gain advantage. After all, process has no feelings. Therefore, if we feel momentum then what does it mean, and what is it worth?

Like watching great quarter-backs tell their football teammates, *"We are now into the two minute drill, and we are down by 10 points in the bottom of the 4th quarter. We have to raise our game."* It's so much driven by emotion as are great negotiations that are tipped by momentum.

We need to incorporate soft, intuitive skills more in sales negotiation. If we sell something with passion, we cannot just turn off the emotional side of our persona when it comes to the negotiation. It just doesn't add up.

So the next time you are engaged in an important business negotiation. Take note of how the other side is reacting to your physical and emotional presence:

1)   Are they quiet and just trying to make it through the negotiation?

2)   Are they anxious and overly talkative?

3)   What kinds of questions are they asking?

4)   How is their eye contact?

5)   How is their body language? Arms folded? Stressed facial expressions?

What does your E.Q. tell you about your negotiation partner? Is there an opportunity staring at us if we can just tap into their needs or help them through a tough bargaining situation? Remember, not everyone hopes to make money on a deal. Some bargaining partners are just as fulfilled by getting a negotiation over with so they can move on the things that they do best.

22

REDUCE STRESS...SAVE ENERGY

Having participated in hundreds of large sales negotiations, I can confidently report no two negotiations are ever completely the same. Businesses change ownership. Senior management teams come and go. Business cultures change trajectory. Category competition changes. Time compresses and decompresses. Budgets fluctuate. Mandates change. Civility changes. In short, trying to accurately predict how a sales negotiation is going to unfold is a little like trying to catch a ball of rolling switchblades. One must prepare, calculate carefully, take precautions, and expect a little stress.

Below are several stress-reducing negotiation tips that have worked for me over and over again. Hopefully, you will find one or two tips that will help you better manage stress during your next major sales negotiation:

1) **Prepare a negotiation planning summary** - In the last days leading up to your next major sales negotiation, compress your planning notes into a summary of bullet thoughts. Get the summary down to a couple of pages. Rank the big money points. Frame your high value questions and trial closes. Highlight the pieces of the negotiation that are critical. This last step of negotiation preparation

will give you a great sense of readiness and relief. It will take some of your stress away because all you could know about the negotiation in the time you had to prepare is now resting in your hands. This fine summary can be read and re-read in just minutes.

2)   **Stay in the present** - The precious present is where all the action is in a big money negotiation. The challenge is not to miss it. We worry about the future and/or get stuck in the past. The present is where you see their body language. You see who defers to whom at the bargaining table. The present is when you catch that wonderful moment when it is time to "pull the pin" and say "yes" to a smartly negotiated deal. You only get to say yes once so don't miss it. Stay in the precious present.

3)   **Practice being underwhelmed** - It is so easy to get caught up in the lumpy noise of a negotiation when the other side does not exactly get what they want and start to rear up. If this happens just relax and practice being underwhelmed. There are negotiators that wait for imperfections in a bargaining session to make unnecessary noise just hoping to knock us off balance. It's a great tactic, but if you know it is coming you simply wait for the noisy tactician to make their point. You address the point, making sure they are heard. You handle the objection and move forward. Don't let them know you even thought it was any more than an explanation of facts or collaborative motive.

4)   **Peddle backwards mentally** - I have found that at times everyone seems to be moving too fast in business negotiations and stress levels elevate unnecessarily. When this happens, I remind myself to visualize that I am riding a 10-speed bike and that I have a choice to peddle backwards. This lets the noisy traffic run past me. In other words – quiet yourself. Don't fill the silence. Let others do the heavy lifting for a while. Visualize that you are peddling backwards while others are racing past you. The irony is that if you do this for a while, collecting your thoughts and analyzing the logic of the moment you will be no further behind when you decide to engage those at the negotiation table again. The difference is that you will be rested and ready to go again. Peddle backwards mentally to reduce stress in business negotiations.

5)   **Meditation & rest** - When you are in the most trying times of a large sales negotiation don't forget to give your brain and body a little time out. Meditate if you can. You can do it anywhere. Rest. Close your eyes and try to think of

nothing or think of a very quiet personal place. Or, think of your family at one of their happiest moments and how loving and peaceful it was. Many top executives these days are taking mini rest breaks. Even a five minute mini break as described above will reduce stress and refresh you when you need it most.

6)   **Laugh, forgive & forget** - A famous Hollywood actress was once asked, *"How do you remain so resilient and successful with all of the strains that go with being an actress?"* She paused and replied, *"I laugh as much as possible. I forgive everyone, and I can't remember a damned thing!"* If someone offends you in a small way in a negotiation just chalk it up to innocent error or crafty gamesmanship. Laugh it off. Forgive and forget. If on the other hand your negotiation partner offends you in a serious way, forgive them, but take note. There is no need for a lack of civility at the bargaining table.

7)   **Dropping your jaw** - When you are feeling seriously stressed, try dropping your jaw one inch and hold it still for a minute. Dropping your jaw will drain all of the tension out of your face and will leave you with a great sense of peace. It works every time.

23

REDUCE CONFLICT...FOCUS ON THE END GAME

When I engage business professionals who shy away from business negotiations, conflict appears to be their greatest emotional blocker. The reasons are varied but they include shyness, upbringing (their parents didn't like negotiating), conservatism and even religion to a degree.

The challenge with this line of thinking is there will always be negotiation either at home with your families or in business with your colleagues or customers. There are techniques to increase effectiveness in business negotiation while reducing conflict.

Conflict for the sake of conflict is just noise. Reduce the noise with quiet, deliberate thought process and you can change the trajectory of the conversation from conflict to a series of well-placed queries. This approach has the potential to be every bit as effective in business negotiations and is really more strategic than tactical. There is room for many styles of thinking and communication at the bargaining table. Some of the brightest negotiators in history have been known to be passive in tone but passionate at heart. Quiet does not mean weak.

Below are six conflict reducing techniques to consider as you head into your next big business negotiation:

1)   **Clearly identify what you need** - If there is one mistake I see business negotiators make it is that they are somewhat sure but not totally sure what they actually need to get a deal done.   This is frustrating for both sides in a negotiation because this lack of clarity eats up valuable time and it can raise the odds of conflict.   I recommend anyone heading into a business negotiation rank their needs and express each need whether in hard or soft costs as a dollar amount.

2)   **Understand their needs** - If you do not take the time to do due diligence to find out what your negotiation partner needs, you are clearly not respecting their position and are inviting unhealthy discussion.   Understanding your negotiation partner needs will help you clearly identify the gap in your two bargaining positions and will bring the possibility of positive collaboration into play.

3)   **Assemble "Money Questions"** - Money questions are another way of saying high value questions.   They are questions that cannot be answered with a straight yes or no and require descriptive answers. Questions that begin with who, why, where, when, how and which are money questions.   Assemble and rank your money questions. In most cases, you can deliver them in a calm, quiet manner that will not offend.   In many instances, this question process lets your bargaining partner know you are sincere about completing a deal.   Each money question you get answered will help build a picture in your mind as to how you can produce a positive conclusion to your business negotiation.

Here are a few money question examples:

a)   What is the highest value retention brand you sell?

b)   Which models require the least amount of servicing?

c)   If I was your sister… what advice would you give me about this deal and why?

d)   Who in your organization would most likely approve my offer?

4)   **Handle objections by hearing them out** - We all want to be heard.   This is especially true in business negotiations.   As soon as you sense the other side is feeling frustrated or venting a little, take steps to lessen conflict.   Just stop and

listen. Take notes. Repeat their objection or frustration in your own words. Let them talk this frustration through. If you are seriously paying attention to them it will help defuse and neutralize them. Ask them to recommend solutions to the perceived problem. Not only are they being heard…they may just warm up to your calm, quiet business acumen. And…best yet, they may actually come up with a positive, accretive solution you had not thought of yourself. You don't have to totally agree with their solutions and may continue with your own stance and objectives. Notwithstanding, we all want to be heard. By hearing them out you will gain respect at the bargaining table and build a stronger partnership toward a smart deal.

5)   **Seek collaboration when bargaining** - Collaboration in bargaining is one of the gold standards of business negotiation. When collaborating in a sales negotiation we are opening up our world so the other side can see more of our side. Objectives become more transparent for both sides. Risks in the negotiation become less mysterious and more instructive. Thus, we reduce the opportunity for conflict to manifest. Some call this approach "Win/Win". I prefer to call it… "We All Win". Collaboration requires courage and willingness to remove your company hat to see that teamwork may well lessen conflict. I am a fan of collaboration because it forces us to look at the world from a 360 degree position with more objectivity. Collaborative negotiations are the gateway to long-term business relationships.

6)   **Always have a back-up plan** - I cannot tell you how many times I have seen intelligent business people go into a large business negotiation with only one plan. Not only is this not recommended….it's limp. So much is riding on one outcome that the negotiator loses agility and flexibility. If the single plan is not agreed to by the other side, you are left going back to the drawing board. Or, you have conflict with your negotiation partner. Professional negotiators would rarely consider going into a large bargaining session with only one plan. They always have at least two plans or more ranked by revenue risk and strategic importance. Professional negotiators refer to a back-up plan as a BATNA. If you want to reduce conflict in your next important negotiation quietly go in with a BATNA. Remember introducing quiet, conflict reducing processes in business negotiation is not weak…it's smart. You don't have to be a bully to win.

24

SMARTLY WITHDRAWING FROM A SALES NEGOTIATION

Entering into a negotiation typically means there is great potential for both parties involved. We savor the opportunity of gathering new wind in our business sails and pressing forward into new lucrative waters.

Unfortunately, for reasons generally not known upfront negotiations can stray into territory that at best feels uncomfortable and at worst makes us feel very exposed. The bargaining horizon suddenly looks fraught with danger. So what circumstance would be so pernicious as to make us pull the plug on what we thought was a good opportunity? Below is a short list of negotiation scenarios to be wary of. At this point, we must count up our gains or losses and leave the bargaining table not to return:

1) **Lose/win** - I cannot tell you why, but, some business professionals are so competitive that they lose sight of the fact negotiation is about making both parties feel like they are constructively engaged and not taken to the cleaners financially. The minute you feel that the other side is pressuring you into uncomfortable territory regarding pricing or future opportunities in a deal, stop and think about it. Think hard. Ask yourself if this feels like the bad side of a binary we lose, they

win scenario? If so pause. Call for a timeout. Do not agree to a final deal until you have had time to review your cost modeling and your BATNA.

2) **Lose/lose** - You might think that "we both lose" scenarios are so rare that it could never happen to you. Wrong. Spoiler deals where everyone loses can happen. Think of it this way….what if the other side wants to do a deal with you so you cannot make progress. Your bargaining partner may actually fear you knowing they cannot win with you in the long run. So until they have a better plan they may actually elect to do a deal that does not make them money but actually slows you down. It's sometimes referred to as a strategic negotiation.

3) **Profit** - If your negotiation partner does not respect your need to make a profit then I see this as a big red flag. This is an indicator of "user mentality". On the rare occasion with a new business negotiation partner we may have to open with a test period of our products and services to prove their worth. Even in these circumstances operating without a profit is senseless and weak. Remember, after any test period we must return to normalized profit margins.

4) **Cascade/contagion price erosion** - If normalized profit/price perimeters are not maintained, your company risks what I refer to as a cascade or contagion price erosion. Years ago, I was approached by a large client to lower our insert distribution rates in a specific region. I was advised if I did not comply they would have to consider moving to our competitor. Against incredible pressure within my own company I withdrew from that proposal for fear of price erosion on this account and others of its size. Years later, I was vindicated and actually congratulated for my courage in taking this unpopular price stance with one of the world's largest retailers.

5) **Ethics/values** - If you feel like you want to take a shower after a bargaining session with a customer or vendor, your stomach is talking to you. On the issue of ethics and values, always listen to your gut. At the very least, refer to your company's ethics and values policy. Once you have crossed the line on constructive bargaining or in the deep water of dubious ethics and values, it is very hard to swim to terra firma. It is hard to undo bad judgment.

6) **Legalities** - I can tell you without question the easiest deals to withdraw from are the ones that bring negative legal implications/exposure into play. Don't go there. A long business career is to be treasured not wasted on short term gain.

25

THE VALUE OF STORYTELLING

An important phase after framing the architecture of a sales negotiation is storytelling. Participating in the media sales business for over 30 years, I observed some absolute masters of storytelling. Storytelling as a skill cannot be underestimated. Having the ability to bring history, creative ideas, risk assessment, cost modeling and logic under one common, sticky theme is artistry.

Storytelling is one of those topics eternally attached to business negotiation and I could simply talk about for hours. I have great stories of wit, cunning, strategy and courage at the bargaining table.

The question is, are there natural storytellers? The short answer is some people have natural command of combining soft skills. They think in these terms. They are curious and naturally ask themselves and those around them many questions in rapid succession. And they are good at taking massive amounts of data and compressing it into a flowing stream of thought, including, the anticipation of crafty negotiation objection busters.

Can storytelling be learned? The short answer is yes. Is there an identifiable structure to storytelling germane to business negotiation? My answer is… storytelling is a personal style unique to us all. Notwithstanding, I will offer what

I believe are nine essential parts of storytelling that you can start with and add to as you grow your storytelling skills. Storytelling is like building a pyramid. There is a base that builds on another base rising until we arrive at a perfect peak.

Here are nine levels of storytelling. Each builds on the next. They are dynamic so you can mix and match them to make them authentic to your unique, effective, storytelling style:

1) **Our businesses** - The history of our businesses is a treasure trove of information to help build a bridge in a business negotiation. To point, a media company I worked for (The Southam Newspaper Group) was established in 1877 in Canada. One of my largest negotiation partners in media contracts was the Hudson's Bay Company (Department Stores) established in 1670 in Canada as a fur trading company. Can you imagine the amount of material I had to access to draw story telling parallels between our two companies? Can you imagine how many bridges to success were built by these two businesses over a hundred plus years? Believe me it is a great story.

2) **Our backgrounds** - Each negotiator at a bargaining table has a different background, heritage, lineage, education and set of life experiences. It's amazing to sit and listen to a negotiation partner for the first time. It is like a door opens to a new world. A world filled with untold and yet to be heard stories that will bring the two business negotiators closer together.

3) **Our interests/objectives** - When two business negotiators arrive at a bargaining table they each have a list of interests and objectives. These objectives and interests no matter how close or how far apart are the germ for a storyline that is in development. And, these stories are catalogued and remembered by the brightest minds in their respective industries, for future reference in bargaining.

4) **Our aspirations/goals** - Each negotiator at the bargaining table has deeper aspirations and goals than are illustrated in a single negotiation. It has to do with building a career and a body of work. Our work will be remembered and referenced by those that follow us. In building a career there is nothing more exciting than telling the story about how you landed the big deal. It could also be how you shared your vision with your negotiation partner for the future and how this positively shaped the spirit of business negotiations that followed.

5)   **Our curiosity** - Our inquisitiveness about our negotiation partner is the gateway to understanding what influences them in good times and under extreme pressure.   Our questions directed to our bargaining partner also give us the threads on which to build a lasting collaborative relationship.   Negotiators who feel a sense of ease and trust will do more constructive deals together. The fun part is these partners will revel and tell the stories of how they managed those negotiations for years to come.

6)   **Our inclusiveness/empathy** - Trust is one of the hardest things to build in a sales negotiation. Yet, it is one of the most important factors in how our negotiation partners view us and our conviction to follow through with our end of a finely crafted deal. If we are not seriously listening to the other side's story, trying to feel their needs, aspirations and even pain, we are not showing empathy. Even worse, we are not really including them in our world beyond getting a signature on a contract.   If you want trust in a negotiation you must listen to the storyline from the other side. Restate this story in your own words so your negotiation partner is assured that they have been heard and that your words are trustworthy.

7)   **Our visualization/end game** - Our visualization for the complete end-to-end motion of a business negotiation is tantamount to success. The trick is to build in storylines to enhance your ability to handle objections and the gentle massaging of ranked BATNA's.   Our ability to tell the story of how we creatively arrived at the incentive plan to close a smartly negotiated deal based on our bargaining partner's storyline is pure symmetry. It is art.   When it closes with broad smiles, it is the end game.

8)   **Our dedication** - When brilliant negotiators close mind boggling deals it does not happen without days/weeks of planning and rehearsal.   When Winston Churchill was getting ready to deliver one of his moving speeches to other world leaders to negotiate the best deals he could with limited leverage during World War II, he practiced feverishly on his family and colleagues.   Most people think Winston was a natural when it came to storytelling.   Winston certainly was a prolific writer but more importantly he was a great strategist who left no detail unturned.   One of Winston's greatest strengths was his ability to script and un-script with ease.   He wove stories with conviction and artistry.   Winston remains one of the greatest negotiators in modern history.

9)   **Our masterful delivery** - How we deliver a storyline during a negotiation is the difference between being seen as weak or strong. It's the difference between being seen as trustworthy or questionable. When you are involved in large business negotiations think about how you want to close out on the deal. What phases or value statements do you want to punctuate? What numbers do you want your negotiation partner to react to positively? What will your final words be in what must be a truly compelling story for closing a smart deal that will last the test of time?

Question? Who is the greatest negotiation storyteller in modern history? My unwavering answer is Sir Winston Spencer Churchill. He was a storytelling genius. He helped save the world during World War II, one great spine tingling speech at a time in an era where there was only radio to tell the unfolding story to the masses in real time. This illustrates the value and the power of storytelling.

26

Tips For Handling Aggressive Negotiators

The majority of business negotiations are generally collaborative, creatively challenging and constructive. Let's be honest, if we have been summoned to the bargaining table we are there representing our company for good reason. We have resources to help create bridges for our negotiation partner to reach their goals and objectives.

Pretty straight forward right? NOT SO FAST. WHAT IF YOUR BARGAINING PARTNER IS JUST ABOUT TO GO NUCLEAR?

I cannot tell you why but there are some circumstances that just get the best of even the most seasoned professionals. They can just flip out in what seem like normal bargaining situations. The person who is typically the most logical person in the room suddenly becomes a 10,000 pound gorilla with an attitude. You could list a hundred reasons why negotiation partners come off the rails and go ballistic. Here, I offer up my top four explanations:

1)   Change

2)   Exposure/negative Risk

3)   Big Money

4)   Budget Pressures

There are few of us who truly savor change or negative risk in business negotiation channels. So when new objectives and new plans creep into the picture the outcome can be quite mercurial.

When big money is involved, bargainers realize that one wrong move could result in jobs and careers being on the line. Big money makes everyone sweat and so it should. Budget pressures can make everyone ornery at the bargaining table.

Years ago, when working in the newspaper industry I was approached by one of the largest department stores in Canada to lower our rates in a particular market whose rates seemed out of touch with the rest of the country.

In what were constructive discussions with the newspaper in question, we negotiated at a rate slightly lower than their historical rate with this department store. It was however, not as deep as what the customer demanded. The risk was the customer could move their business and use this market as a leverage example to the rest of the industry.

Just moments before I was to meet with the customer I received a call from the same newspaper executive, *".... just want you to know your decision to lower these rates will be responsible for two job losses on this end."* Click. It was a short call. Talk about pressure I didn't need.

Still reeling from the angry call from the newspaper, I sat with the customer and presented our case for lowering rates as the client had requested. The rates were not what they had hoped for. Not three minutes into this negotiation, the customer stood up red faced and stomped around his desk. He threatened to bring in one of the very senior executives down the hall to really work me over.

My head was reeling. I was caught in the middle of what looked like two promising internal and external negotiations that were just melting down like a triple scoop ice cream in a heat wave.

Patrick Tinney

In the end, cooler heads prevailed. I saved both negotiations and both relationships by getting everyone to agree that even though not everyone got what they wanted progress had indeed been made.   These negotiations were unnerving but served as great lessons to me in up-coming aggressive/ confrontational negotiations.

Tips and Lessons Learned:

1) **Don't over react** - If you notice that your bargaining partner is starting to lose it, do not over react.   Let the verbal bluster and frustration blow past you.   If you react, the situation could escalate.   Don't let this happen.

2) **Listen and acknowledge** - When our negotiation partner is distressed and unloads on us it is best to listen and acknowledge their frustration.   Everyone wants to know they have been heard.   Once heard the other side will be more open to hearing our BATNA plan.

3) **Separate people from issues** - Issues get solved at negotiation tables not people.   Sometimes people are under so much pressure that they become the opposite of their true selves.   Always take this into account.

4) **Like something about aggressor** - When confronted by an ugly aggressor at the negotiation table, don't let your emotions take over.   If they are using foul verbal or body language as a tool, stop.   Look at your negotiation partner and find something to like about them.   You may even find something humorous about them.   This inner focus on our side keeps us from sliding into the gutter with our negotiation partner.   Again…stick to the negotiation issues, be tight with your BATNA and seek to close a smart deal.

5) **Remain collaborative** - You just never know when a negotiation partner is using guerrilla tactics to see how we operate under pressure. They do this to try to uncover any perceived weakness from us.   If we remain collaborative without moving away from our objectives we are showing enormous strength.   This will gain us respect at the bargaining table.

6) **Think futures** - While we live in the present and are mindful of the past, the future leads to great treasures.   With the rapid turnover in staff these days the person you are negotiating with today could be gone tomorrow.   If you showed great grace under fire it will be generally known within the company you are negotiating with.   Remarkable calmness and stealth generally messes up an

84

aggressor. These same qualities will be a constructive sign to those who follow that we are a professional negotiator not a rookie "truck slammer" easily moved off of our longer view of smart deals that stand the test of time.

27

SALES NEGOTIATION TRAPS TO AVOID

The thing separating great sales negotiators from good sales negotiators is their ability to avoid serious mistakes. If you can eliminate negative risk, you feel more confident about exploring positive risk and push for deals that meet your goals and objectives.

Below are seven of the most important mistakes negotiators make and need to avoid. Sometimes turning a learning opportunity upside down or looking at it backwards helps us learn quicker with deeper insight. Here's hoping you avoid our magnificent seven and become a great negotiator.

Seven important business negotiation traps to avoid:

1)   **Don't assume you know them** - With so much access to information on the internet one has to be astounded by individuals and businesses that do not run deep queries on their negotiation partners. Find out where their company is weak or threatened by competition. Find out where we can leverage our strengths and opportunities based on our unique position in the market. This will add fire to

their needs. It will draw them closer to our needs. The party with the most intelligence at the bargaining table has a huge advantage.

2) **Don't overlook their objectives** - Too often I see business contemporaries head into an important negotiation without concrete ideas of what the other side really wants. This leads to a lot of misfires in opening bargaining positions and can lead to a very wide expectation gap for both negotiation parties. We always want to rank our objectives compared to their objectives by importance and dollar value. How else are we going to establish a back-up plan essential to any profitable negotiation?

3) **Don't rush the numbers** - Financial preparation for business negotiations is called "Cost modeling". The more time we take to become comfortable with the numbers and costs around a negotiation, the clearer our objectives become. This produces confidence. Don't let your negotiating partner rush you into quick business decisions because they are imposing bargaining deadlines. Smart negotiators know compressing time with deadlines during a negotiation can lead the other side to rush their digestion of financials and make snap decisions. This gives smart negotiators more time to focus on their needs and objectives when they are in sight. Given the chance they will close a deal out with you quickly. Win/win is nice. Winning a little more is nicer.

4) **Don't reveal your walk away position** - Professional negotiators will ask piercing questions in a variety of ways to unbalance or distract you into revealing your walk away position. Be alert. Think carefully. Don't give in. Once your negotiation partner knows your walk away position they will bring their entire arsenal of bargaining chips into play to close a deal closest to their objectives. This leaves you just enough incentive to get a deal signed.

5) **Don't forget your BATNA** - If you don't have a back-up plan when negotiating business deals with large customers, you are … 1) Afraid of your negotiation partner 2) Too optimistic 3) Naive or 4) Gambling. Number four Gambling gets our vote. If you don't have a BATNA when negotiating business deals and you are forced into an impasse with a large customer you have nowhere else to go. You are gambling. It's all or nothing. Not only do you potentially lose the deal and a large customer…you have to find a new customer just to break even. Don't ever forget your BATNA.

6)   **Don't continue to sell once you have a deal** - If you get agreement on a deal with a negotiation partner, conclude the meeting quickly and gracefully. Leave on a positive note.   Every extra word you utter to your negotiation opponent after you conclude a deal has the potential to cost you money.   One of my buyer colleagues used to purposely let his negotiation sales partners get so close to deals when the deals were basically done and then just stop. He would let time hang in the air.   He would just stare away and start muttering until the other side asked if they could help with his perceived dilemma.   My colleague referred to this deadening of time as…"The bonus round".   He knew he could usually squeeze another concession out of the other side after the deal was largely done if he could just keep them talking and selling.

7)   **Don't relinquish control of contract content** - The person who drafts a negotiation contract is in control over how each issue in the negotiation gets positioned on paper. They also have the ability to interpret events in the negotiation that were generally agreed upon but could have been perceived as somewhat nebulous.   In other words, the person who drafts the contract gets to write the history of the negotiation as they saw it.   If the other party in the negotiation does not cross this version of history out on the contract and rewrite it then the first version of the contract stands. If both parties sign off they are compelled to honor the contract.   So, if your side gets the chance to draft the contract in any business negotiation they are involved in...Do it.

PART IV - PREPARING TO CLOSE

28

From Better To Best

When watching professional athletes in the moments before they are about to deliver truly great physical performances, they seem to drift into their own quiet mental space. They block the rest of their surroundings out. They proceed into a state of visualization. They are taking years of training and hard work....breaking all this information down into a few thoughts to allow them to focus on their entire performance from start to finish. Professional sales negotiators at the top of their game do exactly the same.

Visualization of the entire negotiation is not only an imperative for them; it is the formula that elevates these business professionals from better to best. Using this unique end to end thinking, they are able to zero in on components of the negotiation that will offer them advantage and options not always perceptible to their negotiation partners.

When professional negotiators quietly visualize before a large business negotiation begins they have a mental checklist of advanced learning. This experience, training and past success allows them to compress massive amounts of intricate information into a few easily accessible buckets. Below are planning and action buckets professional negotiators access and calibrate while in the heat of a bargaining session:

1)   **Risk philosophy** - One of the ways to solidify your end-to-end thinking in an upcoming negotiation is to have risk perimeters that will not be compromised. Predetermine how you are going to curtail negative risk. Conversely, set goals to increase positive risk in the name of getting a bigger, better value piece of the negotiation pie. We want to do this while getting a smart deal done with long standing business partners.

2)   **Process** - We always build process into our forward thinking because it is a road map and a compass if bargaining becomes noisy, lumpy or confusing. If the negotiation doesn't look or sound right we can always go back to our process and ask… "so where are they trying to take us and where are we in the process?" This adjustment of thinking will almost always produce a clear picture of pieces of the puzzle that are missing or purposely being hidden by the other side.

3)   **Objectives** - Clearly understand the gap between our objectives and those of our bargaining partner will take much of the guess work and most of the unwanted surprises out of our negotiation. This puts us in a position to confidently plan our course of action.

4)   **Strategy alignment** - Whether we know it or not we all work with some type of strategy in a business negotiation. Some business people cannot describe their strategy. Others just call it counter punching…waiting for the other side to act first. At Centroid Training we like to think about the strategy that will not only be effective, but, enticing to the other side. If our strategy is not producing the results we were expecting in the negotiation, then we simply switch gears and move into one of several other strategies. We do this to complement our partner's approach to bargaining while steadfastly matching our objectives to the negotiation.

5)   **Tactical responses** - When the other side is using a wide array of tactics to push us out of our comfort zone how do we plan to respond? Grace under fire is key, but, more importantly can we look beyond the clever or obtuse tactic and see where they are trying to maneuver us? This is what we want to understand and this is what will drive our tactical response to theirs. This is the high stakes poker part of the negotiation.

Patrick Tinney

6)   **ZOPA patience** - Waiting for just the right moment to invite our bargaining partner into the "Zone Of Potential Agreement" cannot be understated. If we look anxious, expect them to take advantage of this moment. If the cadence of our voice or our body language changes, they may pick up on it and slow events down to frustrate us into making mistakes. Be cool. Be smart. Be patient. Wait for the right moment to move into the ZOPA.   Remember we can politely say no a thousand times without offending the other side but once we say yes…we own it.

7)   **BATNA flexibility** - Flexibility around our 'Best Alternative To A Negotiated Agreement" is grounded in knowing our profitability. This combined comfort in long term pricing and value incentives makes us agile. The more comfortable we become in this space, the more exacting we are in cutting a compelling deal at just the right moment without hesitation.

8)   **Control** - The two things we want to visualize having command over in a negotiation are the tempo of the negotiation and the content of the final agreement. If you can maneuver tempo you are driving the discussion. If you have command over the final content of the contract or agreement you will be able to tuck in the unspoken parts of the negotiation in your own language.

29

WHY BATNA IS SUCH A POWERFUL TOOL

In a cooperative negotiation with an important customer, the tendency is to believe, we will both come to the negotiation table with our best ideas. The outcome has to be obvious, constructive and accretive for both sides. It sounds great however, life is not fair and brilliantly crafted sales proposals can fall flatter than a pancake at the bargaining table. This is where a BATNA comes in. The acronym BATNA stands for "Best Alternative to a Negotiated Agreement". Simply, BATNA means back-up plan or a stream of back-up plans. BATNA can have dozens of different components. Your imagination sets the outer limits.

Below is a list of BATNA components I find are almost always in the fore:

1)   **Creative solutions** - Customers buy creative ideas not stuff. The more that we can appeal to a client need or aspiration with a unique creative solution we add tremendous value with our BATNA.

2)   **Proposal incentives** – BATNA incentives may be back loaded or front loaded with cash or product incentives. The larger questions are as follows. Is the incentive meaningful to the client? How does it help them build their business?

How does it help them save money? How does this incentive solidify and grow our position with the client?

3)   **Cost modeling** - Price and profitability are cornerstones of cost modeling. We have to be sure we are striking a balance with these elements. A volume based negotiation with no profit is hollow and potentially damaging to our overall business.

4)   **Value instruments** - We can find deep value in a lot of the systems, research and licenses we pay for on an annual basis. Remember, if we take a low value internal operation for granted it does not mean our customer will. In many cases, they will jump at the chance to try something out of their budgetary reach for free or a reduced cost.

5)   **Quality variables** - The integrity and depth of a product is in the eye of the beholder. Moving quality variables up or down to meet a client's needs may seem small to us but maybe a god sent to them in a nimble BATNA.

6)   **Time variables** - Elasticity in a BATNA often comes down to how we use and perceive time. In my days in the media business, I wanted to use all of the "off-shift" printing time I could find as a tool to lower pricing on printing. It may sound like a cliché but time really does often mean money.

I will leave you with two last tips.

When presenting a proposal with unit costs, total costs and percentage point channels remember that not all of us see numbers the same way. When it comes to presenting a percentage point gain or reduction not everyone calculates the outcomes with the same speed and accuracy.

Finally, remember when presenting your BATNA try to visualize that you are in a round room so that even as you back up and maneuver you are never confined to a corner.

30

OPPORTUNITY SALES OBJECTIONS

Opportunity objections in a sales negotiation are the gateway to truly understanding what the customer really believes and wants. An opportunity sales objection is also what is standing between us and a great sale of a proposal. An opportunity objection is a blockage to a converted customer who is happy with a sales negotiation and the purchase they are about to make.

If there are no objections in a sales negotiation then we as sales people and negotiators have become nothing more than clerks writing orders that have absolutely no stretch or positive risk associated with them. In other words, we are managing transactions of commoditized products.

Most sales people do not practice handling objections. They try to manage this process by thinking on their feet. By doing so, they are counter punching with customers, packed with personal anxiety using phases such as "we've already thought of that..." This does not take the customers worries away, but rather shelves them. To a degree makes the customer look uneducated for asking a legitimate question with potential personal exposure. Making the customer feel dumb is not a great way to close a sale or build a much needed relationship.

Here is the way to succeed with opportunity objections:

1)   **Listen** - If a customer raises a concern or worry they are doing so to mitigate risk. Listening intensely to our customers is paramount. Don't interrupt. As a customer, if I get the sense my salesperson does not care about my risk, I will slow down the sales process until I feel the risk is in check or worse yet just walk away.

2)   **Rephrase** - By rephrasing the customer's concern or worry we as sales people have acknowledged there is a potential blocker to a sale that must be addressed.   It also means, we a getting a clearer sense of the customer's objectives.

3)   **Empathy** - Letting the customer know we empathize with their worry or concerns brings us closer to them.   It's a relationship builder. It's a trust builder. No amount of money in the world can buy trust.   It must be earned and protected.

4)   **Query** -   Asking well-crafted high value questions will get to the bottom of most concerns. The worry could be safety, financial or past bad experiences. We must uncover the nature of the concern to have any hope of neutralizing it. So if this blockage opens up again the sales and negotiation processes can move forward.

5)   **Creative solutions -** Now that we have a better understanding of our customer's worry by asking great high value questions we can set to work our ability to reshape the offer or proposal to fit the customer's eye.   Think scale, innovation, service, quality, delivery timelines and payment plans.   Leave price as a last resort and use it only if we are profitable.

6)   **Collaboration** - Openly solving problems with a customer is the pinnacle of consultative selling.   It signals the customer and salesperson are opening up their minds to arrive at a greater good and fulfillment for both.   Collaboration is actually the "green shoot" of a future and profitable transaction.

7)   **Our POD** - Our ability to truly express our "Point of Difference" at this stage of solving opportunity objections is what will separate us from our competitors.   Our POD also has the ability to reduce commoditization.

8)   **Benefits** - When addressing an opportunity objection and having explored the core of the customers concerns or needs with an array of solutions, we are now able to talk about benefits.   Not just any benefits.   They must connect us emotionally to the customer. They must make them feel safer, more creative, smarter, more efficient, relaxed and or less exposed.   Think of these benefits as benefits on steroids.

9)   **Trial close** - If as a top level sales person you have guided your concerned customer through her/his opportunity objection using the above process you are ready and the customer is primed for a trial close.   See if the sale and negotiation can now be closed with a question such as "valued customer…when and where would you like to begin to enjoy this great program?"

31

SALES NEGOTIATIONS, PLUS TIME, EQUALS MORE MONEY

In sales negotiation, time is the wild card. It doesn't favor buyers or sellers, yet it has the potential to favor either. In the sales world, we refer to the shortening of time as "Time Compression". It stands to reason then that the lengthening of time is "Time Decompression".

"Time Compression", as a tactic, is more challenging to the party that is on the receiving end of it. It means the party you are engaging is forcing you in some way to show your negotiation hand and in some cases make a decision.

For sellers, the shortening of time can be used to separate buyers from tire kickers.

A seller could state:

1)   "First come first served…"

2)   "For a limited time only…"

3)   "We need your decision now…"

The buyer can similarly use time compression to their advantage stating:

1)   "We'll make our decision shortly…"

2)   "We're going to make this purchase within 24 hours…"

3)   "We're going to chat among ourselves and make a decision   now…"

As a buyer or a seller, I just love time compression because it brings all parties in a sales negotiation to the moment of truth. It's "speak now or forever hold your peace."

Time Compression Example

You could use the following time compression exercise and example for almost any large ticket purchase where there are several sales outlets or sale channels for an identical product.   For this example we are using an automobile purchase.

We use time compression to our advantage in a strategy we call "The Auction".

In the auction automobile example, we visit three car dealerships knowing exactly what car, model and features we want.   We tell the salesperson we engage we are going to buy a car in 24 hours.   We also tell them we are going to visit two other car dealerships and no "offer" details between the other car dealers will be shared.

We request their best price now but, we request that they remain profitable in formulating their deal.   Once the three dealership offers are submitted to us, the losing bids will be called and told they did not succeed. That's all. The winning dealership gets the congratulatory call and we sign the deal.

Time decompression is more subtle and has a much wider range for application and affect for both the buyer and seller.

Time Decompression Example

In my view, there was no one better at using the subtle nuances of time decompression than Steve Cosic, former Director of Media Procurement for The Hudson's Bay Company in Canada.

Steve had a number of great proposals presented to him weekly by media suppliers. Each proposal presented would get his deep scrutiny.   More often than not he would pause after what could be seen as a buying signal from him to many of us.

He would just pause, and wait, and start to mutter to himself or shuffle paper on his desk. He wouldn't fill the silence until the seller would say something such as *"Steve, you seem hesitant. What would it take to close this deal?"* To which Steve would reply, *"What do you have in mind?"*

The seller would reveal one more sweetener to the tabled proposal and Steve would often sign the deal.

Many years later after leaving his role, Steve Cosic would reveal that beautifully placed time delays of silence (time decompression) yielded tons more extra value for his employer and that he lovingly called that last delay to purchase "The Bonus Round."

32

NAVIGATE THE BARGAINING CONTINUUM

In the early development stages of Centroid Training and Marketing, I had great fortune to meet a bright MBA graduate we'll call Cheryl. She was a strong, clear-eyed, business person wise beyond her years.

We discussed and dissected several business negotiation tactics and strategies. She offered her MBA view of the world and that of growing up working in a successful family manufacturing business.

While building Centroid Training, I documented well over a dozen effective negotiation strategies and had attached useful business metrics to measure them. As we debated negotiation strategy we finally got to the very common "Split the Difference" strategy.

"Oh I know that strategy too well" said Cheryl with great gravitas. *"There is an old buyer my Dad has been selling to forever. He comes to our offices and low balls our manufacturing lines. He tells my Dad he doesn't have much money and uses a lot of not so nice tactics to get Dad feeling sorry for him. Eventually, it turns into a messy debate about price until finally this buyer says let's split the*

difference ...c'mon help me out.   Dad in his frustration with this old buyer takes the deal almost every time."

The Bargaining Continuum can be tough to navigate at the best of times.   Cheryl wishes her Dad could see it and just say "no" to the split the difference negotiation strategy.

The complicating factor with this case is the old buyer is actually using two strategies in tandem.   He is using the "Poor Mouth"…I really like your products but I just don't have enough money strategy.   This negotiation strategy grinds on some people to the point where the seller just wants to put an end to the melodramatic discussion.   The old buyer waits until he sees a moment of frustration on the sellers face and then he applies the "Split the Difference" strategy.   These two strategies under the right conditions are an insidious one-two, knock-out punch.

As we enter the Bargaining Continuum (also known as ZOPA or Zone of Potential Agreement) most business negotiation partners can generally see the net difference in each other's cost objectives and work toward reciprocity where both imagine a profitable price and fulfilling deal.

If however, we draw a negotiation partner into the Bargaining Continuum with a price that is very far from our partner's price it sets up potentially volatile exchanges.   If neither party moves toward reciprocity and I say "let's just split the difference" I am effectively discounting your offered price by a wide margin.

Here's the trick, with the split the difference strategy as you enter the Bargaining Continuum…we always want to control the split price.   If we do not control the split price we are going to get taken to the cleaners.

Split the difference is versatile in that the split can be useful to drag prices up or drag them down.   If I am a seller, using split the difference, I will drag them up harvesting more price yield.   If I am a buyer and a drag the split down I am asking for a deep discount on top of the quoted seller price.

If a bargaining partner tries to draw you into the Bargaining Continuum with a split the difference strategy….here are a few things you can do to blunt their efforts:

1)   Call for a time out to analyze and cost model the split the difference offer

2)   Call the other side for using split the difference to create a Win/Lose outcome

3)   Stop negotiating and recommend a new strategy to recognize both partner needs

4)   Walk away if your negotiation partner is not vital to your business

The above four points work toward neutralizing your negotiation partner if you are drawn into a split the difference reciprocation sequence in the Bargaining Continuum.

The moment you hear split the difference, stop and think the situation through carefully. Be cautious. Review your cost model again. Review your back up plans. Avoid the obvious canard and restart the negotiation if you are not comfortable.

33

Use Smart Sales Negotiation Tactics

Sales negotiation tactics are the theatre of the mind tactics that can be quite subtle and intellectual. They can be "carney like" reminding us of bad infomercials or captivating parlor tricks. In the right setting, tactics can be used to unbalance and or confuse the other side.

The challenge for many who engage in sales negotiation is to truly understand the significance of using tactics. Tactics help shape a positive business negotiation relationship, environment and most importantly, a solid strategy. Tactics are designed to close smart, fulfilling deals for both negotiation partners.

When I ask business people how they negotiate or more directly ask them to name their top two business negotiation tactics or strategies…more times than not, I get vague answers.

This tells me that many business people who negotiate on behalf of their families and their company are in one of several camps:

1)   They do not prepare enough for the negotiation

2)   They are not well trained in business negotiation

3)   They rely too much on gut instinct and situational analysis

4)   They just lack confidence in their ability to negotiate

All of the above can be very costly over the long run.

Many people view business tactics as the strategy.   They do this without realizing that tactics should be the lighting and sound effects around a great screen play. The ultimate goal of the play is to bring the viewer and participant to a moving and emotive crescendo. This will result in a personal experience of fulfillment, approval and comfort.

Early in my career of selling and negotiating media contracts, I worked with a newspaper colleague who used passionate negotiation tactics to gain the upper hand on negotiation partners.   He was an Advertising Director at a large Canadian daily newspaper.   He was revered by customers and colleagues for his ability to get tough deals done.

Without doubt he was one of the most flamboyant business negotiators in the media industry of his era.   In one mercurial business negotiation he pulled out all stops.

A home renovation customer had a penchant for picking away at our newspaper run of press advertising yields.   The customer made so many changes on their newspaper advertising proofs that it was almost impossible to get the changes perfect.   Weekly negotiations would take place on compensation to be paid to the home renovation customer.

Larger negotiations were required.   A meeting was arranged.   Three of us represented the newspaper sales team. Three represented the home renovation customer. At this meeting the home renovation company owner was quietly engaged in convivial conversation with my manager.   I was speaking to their advertising manager in positive tones.

My Advertising Director and the General Manager for the home renovation company who was famous for his voluminous advertising proof changes sat staring at each other.   This went on for many uncomfortable minutes.   Finally, our Ad Director looked directly into the General Manager's eyes and said *"I know you don't like me…and I want you to know I really don't like you…but before we leave you and I are going to get a deal done."*

Our Advertising Director and the customer's General Manager were using both physical and verbal negotiation tactics to gain bargaining table image and to appear as the alpha negotiator. Both were using tactics to unbalance each other. Both were using tactics to show a test of will. To this day, I honestly believe they both thoroughly enjoyed the experience.

Our Advertising Director using speed tactics to impress with a huge big button calculator was punching away at what he believed was going to be a great deal to end the bickering. He wanted to grow our newspaper advertising revenue and firmly reset the business relationship for both companies. As he slashed away at his calculator he came to an eye popping proposal and proudly presented it to the customer on the spot. Big smiles from both sides. Big hand-shakes from all involved. We left the meeting deal done.

Now back at the newspaper, my phone rings…it's the Advertising Director. He said *"Paddy, Paddy, Paddy. Quick, come over to my office."* He was sitting there re-crunching all the numbers in the home renovation proposal and shaking his head back and forth. He couldn't believe it, the numbers didn't add up.

Unbelievably, the negotiation with the home renovation company had to start all over again.

You can only imagine the negotiation tactics that ensued.

Note to self, plan your negotiation tactics and always, always have a back-up plan.

34

BEWARE OF LEAKY STRATEGIES

Recently, I had quotes ordered for a set of windows, I was replacing at my home. With quote appointments in place, the first window company representative arrives. He looked at the job and asked how many other window companies would be quoting? He also wanted to know if he was first or last in the quote sequence. When I told him he was first he got very annoyed and did not want to quote. He said *"Call me back when the others have quoted and I will quote"*. I queried…*Why*? He said *"Once we review the other quotes, I will then quote and we will do a deal."*

I told him to quote on the spot or just leave. He quoted and I told him his sales negotiation strategy was weak and obtuse. His negotiation strategy is what we refer to as a "share and compare" in the world of business negotiation. Ultimately, he did not win the job simply because I no longer trusted that his business acumen and the quality of his work would satisfy my future needs.

You might think obtuse sales negotiation strategies such as "share and compare" are a rarity in large corporate business negotiations. Sadly, not so.

Patrick Tinney

The problem for corporate sellers is there will always be a new low in price as new competitors appear. The new suitor will promise the world in quality and timing. And, they will deliver the product at a new lower price.

Once the new low price hits the market…it leaks and the former seller will tear at the contract carcass trying to solve the price problem and assess future profitability.

I am reminded of a similar situation I once experienced.

I was made aware by a client we'll call "WXYZ" that one of my competitors was quoting him on a piece of business we held with a new low, low price in Western Canada.

I reviewed our cost modeling and knew that the business was not profitable at the new competitor low, low price. I also knew that our delivery systems and brand were stronger than what my competitor was claiming.

We reviewed our BATNA and made several creative pitches to WXYZ. We presented variations on our core and supplemental products to make up the difference but WXYZ was fixated on price. We could not match the price and be profitable. Furthermore, if we accepted the new low price and essentially bought our business back, this low rate could leak into the market. It could have a cascade effect with the rest of our accounts further pushing revenue down.

Worse yet, this "share and compare" negotiation strategy was taking place in a clustered geographic setting. Contiguous markets could also be affected. Share and compare had the potential to drive revenue down across the whole province.

Our company senior managers on the scene were howling. They worried that if they lost WXYZ account their world would cave in. They believed they would lose even more business sighting that WXYZ was a bell weather account that would drag many other businesses with them to our local competitor.

There was huge pressure to make the right decision.

Examining all data available, revisiting our BATNA and now looking at the wider picture with this Pan-Canadian account, I held my ground. I told our Western Canadian Team we were walking away from this piece of business based on price exposure nationally.

Several years later, I get a call from a man we'll call Tom (not his real name). He was our newly minted Senior Executive in this same Western Region. The first thing he did in his new role was to review profitability on major accounts.

One account in particular we will call "ABC" had been beaten down on price in negotiations. It had to be addressed. I did not negotiate this ABC deal, but because I was the category manager for the company I was one of Tom's first calls.

"Hello Pat... *"How do we raise the rates on ABC account so we can be more profitable?"* It would be a long process with lots of heavy lifting and lots of hair curling business negotiations.

We then proceeded to discuss the WXYZ situation from years ago and all of the deep cost modeling I had completed on this account. We had been up against great pressure/resistance and ultimately walked away from WXYZ business at the new low, low price.

Tom's response? *"Thank goodness you did your homework and did not buy that business. Just look at the challenges we have now."*

35

NEGOTIATION STRATEGY…IS ONE ENOUGH?

Most of us learned to negotiate while growing up by imitating siblings, classmates and even parents. We watched others get what they wanted pushing the "buttons" of those they were engaging, in a predetermined sequence, at just the right time. It was bubblegum generals … planning kid warfare.

Over time, we develop a series of "go to" bargaining strategies that define us. As parents we often use the "Good Cop/Bad Cop" to keep our offspring in check. That is until our children figure out that the Good Cop is too good and the Bad Cop is just an old softie. Children know that just one well-placed tear running down a cheek gets them everything they ever wanted. And, it leaves the parents scrabbling to determine which one of them caved in first.

The same thing happens in business negotiations. The only difference is, it's not about bubblegum or video game haggling, it's about a contract or deal that could be worth thousands or even millions of dollars.

As professionals engaging in negotiations it is our job to pull the other side toward our list of objectives and get agreement on our needs. This, while listening to the other side and making them feel fulfilled monetarily or emotionally by the outcome of the deal.

One negotiating strategy on its own might get a deal done if your partner has not seen the strategy before or has not bargained with you before. The problem is that after we engage someone a few times we start to predict bargaining outcomes. We look for "tells" (Poker term for Personal Quirks) from the other side. That tips us to the negotiation strategy the other side is using. I remember a contemporary who smiled inappropriately when he would get nervous. He couldn't control it. Watch your "tells".

Centroid Training has identified over 20 different Negotiation Strategies one could encounter in a negotiation.

Professional Negotiators have several tried, true and tested strategies that they mix and match to their partners styles to get the best results. To put it another way "Pros" scope out the playing field and approach each bargaining exercise with a negotiation strategy and a series back up strategies.

They realize that all deals have individual personalities that require interpretation depending on the Needs, Costs, Timing and Style associated with the other side.

Centroid with its negotiation experience has placed risk markers for Buyers and Sellers on Negotiation Strategies. Secondly, we've topped up this Buyer/Seller relationship with a Time Compression risk marker for each strategy.

By selecting pieces of over 20 different strategies for a negotiation it is possible to keep "them" off balance. This gives us maximum opportunity to reduce our negative risk while taking more positive risks to achieve a smart deal while maintaining our relationship.

Before entering into any important deals or contracts where negotiation strategy is required ask yourself… "Is one enough"?

36

LIMITED STRATEGIES LEAD TO LESS PROFIT

Whenever I engage colleagues on the subject of sales negotiation I almost always ask them "…on a scale of 1 to 10, how do you rate yourself as a negotiator?" Invariably, the answer I get is… "Oh I think I'm about 7 out of 10." Some colleagues are more honest and give me another number.

The next question I generally ask is "…So where did you learn to negotiate?"

Most cannot really answer this question so, I help them. I suggest to them that they learned to negotiate by imitating:

1)   Parents

2)   Siblings

3)   Classmates

4)   And finally business co-workers

The net result is most of us tend to gravitate toward two or three negotiation strategies we feel comfortable with. These select strategies work some of the time and or work on people that do not know us.

In the world of professional selling, contract negotiations the above scenario will limit your profit.

A professional negotiator is adept at:

1)   Reconnaissance

2)   Time compression and decompression

3)   Situational analysis

4)   Cost Modeling

5)   Negotiator style identification and so on…

The above skills and others are turned and twisted like a Rubik"s Cube to create a large menu of strategies that can be accessed at will. As a senior sales executive friend of mine recently said, *"negotiation is like a chess game that never ends."*

Those in business without a wider negotiation strategy arsenal live in a narrow business channel. They may miss the opportunity to secure greater value from their negotiation engagements or worse yet be on the bad end of poor deals.

As a sales manager for a large media company, my job was to extract the best value out of our print and delivery products. I had to do this while still maintaining a good working relationship with our customers. In other words, my job was to get a smart deal done and make the other side feel comfortable or fulfilled.

One strategy that more than one customer would use on us was to call our office negotiate the best deal they could and then call our local offices and use our deal to cut a deeper deal. This negotiation strategy is known as "Double Dipping." Once identified we simply neutralized this strategy without the customer   becoming aware.

There are several of these rudimentary strategies that are easy to identify if you are a seasoned business negotiator. The trick is to always neutralize the other side and pull them closer to your objectives and quietly close the deal. Professional negotiators do this securing slightly more than their fair share of the available proceeds in the negotiation.

You do not want the other side to feel poorly in a deal struck. You want them to step away from the bargaining table feeling like they did the best job they could in the negotiation and fulfilled. If you can succeed in helping your negotiation partners find this comfort zone, you will profit on a consistent basis in business negotiations.

As I often say to clients… *"What if I could positively change the trajectory of your business negotiations by a single percentage point? What would that mean to your company?"* At larger companies a single percentage point potentially means millions of dollars annually.

So here are a couple of questions. How many different negotiation strategies do your sales teams use on a consistent basis? And, how effective is your team at profiting in business negotiations?

37

THE IMPORTANCE OF FRAMING SALES NEGOTIATIONS

When readying to engage in the last face to face stage of a large sales negotiation it is a mistake to overlook framing the proceedings. Too often, I see neophyte, stressed or harried negotiators rush to crack open negotiations with their bargaining partners without setting the stage for all at the table. It's truly a missed opportunity.

By framing the past, present and future dealings with a customer we have a unique moment to contextualize our intentions and those of our company. In doing so, we also have one last opportunity to check the temperature of the other side for their openness to cooperate and collaborate. If we don't experience cooperative feedback from our bargaining partners expect a longer, thornier bargaining engagement. This last touch with the customer allows us to shift strategic and tactical gears to fit the terrain.

There are a number of ways to frame negotiation however, the subjects below are at the top of our list of must do's. This is our opportunity to be a storyteller of all things good about getting smart deals done that stand the test of time:

Patrick Tinney

1)   **History** - Past bargaining sessions with our negotiation partner can motivate the future. By speaking to the history of our two companies and the successes we have enjoyed, we are able to shine a light on future opportunities.   If this is our first business negotiation, we can elect to profile how our business category regularly conducts and concludes successful cooperative negotiations. The idea is to look for planks to build a solid bridge with our customer.

2)   **Common interests** - By visiting common interests with our negotiation partner, we are laying even more solid planks on our bridge to a successful deal. Common interests may have both monetary and non-monetary implications. Common interests may even include potential community building, philanthropic opportunities.   These community and B2C awareness programs create more mutual opportunities as an organic offshoot.

3)   **Common objectives** - In citing common objectives with our negotiation partner we are really asking a question.   We are querying about closure of distance for the larger items in the negotiation such as price, quality and time ("The Big Three").   If when we speak to the other side about "The Big Three" we get positive feedback then, we know entering the bargaining continuum (AKA ZOPA) will be easier.   If however, we get silence or disagreement, rest assured there will be more heavy lifting to get closer to the door of a deal.

4)   **Spirit of agreement** - The spirit of agreement is really a nice way of saying "code of conduct" or "code of common courtesy".   There will either be honor among men (meaning men and women) or their will be honor among thieves.   Whether faced with cooperative bargaining or game theory competition, it is always good to know there will be a framework for overcoming obstacles and blockages in a professional manner.

5)   **Mutual opportunity** - During the framing process it is good to try to get a measurement for everyone to have a meaningful piece of opportunity.   When framing this part of the negotiation if we get a sense from the other side that the deal will be lopsided in their favor it is the time to suggest that we look at a bigger pie.   By expanding the opportunity for both parties the negotiation takes shape giving our side the incentive and fortitude to conclude a fulfilling and constructive deal.

6)   **Determination** - There is a strong correlation between momentum and determination in successfully closing a large sales negotiation. When framing a large negotiation we really want to hear from the other side that they will see it through.   We want to know that we will both have "puts and calls" that will need to be addressed and successfully navigated with everyone's interests taken into consideration. If at this point, you get a limp response from the other side, you may be in trouble.   If the other side is affirmative and enthusiastic you are ready to go. And, well on the way to closing another smart, accretive deal.

There may be some out there who think framing sales negotiations in the final stages of a bargaining session too theatrical or a waste of time.   To those I say…a deal is not a deal until the goods have been delivered and we have been paid in full. I would also say that poorly crafted deals are bound to leak oil or may be unreliable in the delivery phase.   So my friends frame your deals smartly.   Tell the other side they matter and that you care.   Tell them everyone deserves to make a profit.

38

BE CREATIVE WHEN WEAK

Negotiating from a position of weakness happens to us all on a daily, weekly or monthly basis.   Negotiating from a weak stance happens for a variety of reasons:

- Scarcity

- Time compression or decompression

- Lack of knowledge

- Lack of technology

- Lack of funds

- Fear

- And others…

Winston Churchill may have been the greatest negotiator from a position of weakness in modern history.   He understood the above reasons for smart negotiation from a weak stance and he made the most of it.

Modern business and political diplomacy learned a lot from Sir Winston and his battle against the Axis of Evil in World War II. Owing to Churchill's superb decision making process and brilliant tactics/strategy in negotiating with The USA, USSR, France and his own countrymen what have we garnered?

We can negotiate smarter from a position of weakness if we observe just a few of the following stratagems Churchill employed:

1)	**Appear strong** - This has to be the oldest stratagem ever, however, it makes the other side think twice. Remember the quote from Churchill's famous World War II speech, *"We shall defend our island, whatever the cost may be, we shall fight on the beaches, we shall fight on the landing grounds, we shall fight in the fields and in the streets, we shall fight in the hills; we shall never surrender."* This speech put Britain's enemies on notice. We can do the same with our negotiation partners but in less bellicose terms.

2)	**Show leadership. Propose solutions** - In his time of dire need Churchill ground out more proposals for help for his British people than imaginable. At times, Winston had multiple secretaries working two shifts a day. By doing so, he was taking control of the narrative. He was opening negotiation discussions on his terms and scope. When in a weak negotiation position we must ask ourselves…in spite of the tough spot we are in, is it not wiser to be in the tent driving toward the end game?

3)	**Build partnerships** - Strategic partnerships are paramount for poorly positioned negotiators. Britain was being smashed by the German Air Force and its Naval Submarine Command. The United Kingdom's food sources were being sunk to the bottom of the Atlantic. The British faced the possibility of starvation. Churchill needed The USA to join The British in the War against Hitler. Churchill wrote, called out to and cajoled Franklin D. Roosevelt (FDR) then USA President to help save the British and The World. Just prior to the bombing of Pearl Harbor FDR moved toward Churchill in offering more than just materials and food. It was a long negotiation, years in the making. So, remember Winston, when you are in a tough spot in a business negotiation and need to develop a strategic partnership. Tip? Do not rule out your competitors as potential negotiating partners.

4)   **Sell futures** - With the British Empire breaking up and on the way to bankruptcy, Churchill negotiated key land rights for naval bases with President Roosevelt. Both leaders were negotiating future opportunities. Churchill put in play one of his last negotiation chips to keep his country afloat. When businesses of all stripes face late payments or a financial squeeze the first thing they do is negotiate futures. Think about how many companies Warren Buffett negotiated with in the 2008 financial crisis on the basis of these companies selling futures. It was a Win/win.

5)   **Admit strategic weakness** - Churchill secretly admitted Britain's military and economic weaknesses to FDR while boldly telling Hitler that if the Nazi's invaded Britain …the "Brits" would fight to the last person. This confession of weakness to a potential negotiation partner showcased Churchill as a savvy negotiator and a leader to be trusted. In key negotiations from a position of weakness, imagine the courage it took for Churchill to pull the curtain back. Remember Winston. Be smart and save your negotiation.

6)   **Get creative. Innovate.** – As World War II progressed Britain's factories, buildings and homes were being bombed to rubble. Materials and food were being sunk by Nazi submarines. England however, was innovating and looking for a new edge. The English were working on an infantile experiment with the idea of combining bomb mentality, fusion science and uranium. Part of Britain's creative negotiation for more supplies was its Atomic Bomb Science which it shared in full with The United States. Question? In a weak negotiation position, how will your company add hidden value with your creative innovations?

7)   **Sell fear/bullying** - Safe to say Churchill was brilliant in alarming the world that Hitler was unjustly invading his neighboring countries with a much wider and more monovalent plan in mind. I can tell you from personal experience if you want to mess up a large company you are negotiating with…just tell them you feel like you are being bullied with their tactics and that their course of business is preventing you from making money. Especially, if you can get to a VP/C Suite Officer of the company you are negotiating with. These executives cringe at a bullying narrative because it casts a noisy light upon them. Remember, senior executives do not like noisy issues that are sticky. Many will fold like a tent and become very conciliatory if you know how to gently push their hot buttons.

When negotiating from a weak position remember Winston Churchill. Never give in.

39

Negotiating Via Mobile, Skype Or E-Mail

Increasingly, the business community is breaking away from face-to-face negotiation and moving these critical engagements to Mobile, Skype or e-Mail. When we strip away the ability to make direct eye contact with a negotiation partner we lose one of most valuable EQ measurement tools. When we cannot see the person's body movements or cannot reach over and touch them. The conversation takes on many new dynamic tones. This opens up all kinds of mine fields regarding how our motives are being viewed and interpreted by our negotiation partners. Some buying and procurement groups are using e-Mail as a firewall or vendor fact checking tool. They send out RFP's (Request For Proposals) knowing that this information will be used to keep their current preferred vendors in check or worse under cost pressure.

We could discuss this topic at length however, below are my ten best tips when negotiating using either mobile, Skype or e-Mail:

1)   **Be proactive** - I like to be the person initiating the call to the other side. This is important as it gives me greater time to get my ducks in order. There is nothing worse than being pulled out of an important business moment and then

suddenly being plunged into a negotiation. Think of how many times a customer calls up with a budget they want to spend. They pull you out of another deep engagement that is eating up all of your mental and emotion energy. It takes great agility and concentration to pull oneself into the present new opportunity.

2) **Preparation** - It is also important to prepare for this call/email in an extraordinary fashion so, if you get knocked off script or plan you have as many tools around you as possible. And, because our customers are accessing data bases and pulling range reports on pricing it is vital that we keep up-to-date files on past negotiation pricing with all important clients.

3) **Ranked objectives** - There really is money in ranking our objectives before a non-face-to-face negotiation. If we are not focused on the dollar value of each of our objectives in a ranked fashion there is a chance that we may overlook an important objective. Note to self, clarify exactly what the other side needs and match that information up with our needs and look for the opportunity gaps.

4) **Monitor time compression** - Managing time is a beast in non-face-to-face negotiations. The other side can create an atmosphere of urgency by ratcheting up deadlines designed to force decisions quicker than normal. If you feel this type of gamesmanship taking place, slow the negotiation down. Call for a break on the basis that you need time to review your best options on your negotiation partner's best behalf. This pays dividends in the long run.

5) **Cost modeling** - I am a huge fan of cost modeling. Especially, for large or mercurial accounts. When customers are making large expenditures with our company there is an expectation that we are always on top of their account. Secondly, if you know you are dealing with a detailed multi-level negotiation it pays to be able to shift gears between cost models on various products to come up with the best solution possible in a live setting. This is an advanced scenario. Increasingly, as more and more customers avoid face-to-face negotiations, we will be required to make tougher, quicker decisions to hold and grow our share of a customer's budget.

6) **Simple language** - My advice to Centroid Training clients who negotiate using e-Mail, Mobile or Skype is to be very careful with the words we choose. As I mentioned earlier, we cannot see the other side moving their bodies or facial expressions as they react to our responses to their queries. Avoid any temptations

to fit in a joke or a glib remark as these actions can just totally derail a constructive discussion.   Stay with the facts and listen more than you speak.

7)   **Control your emotions** - Never let them see the whites of your eyes. Even if you are anxious, frustrated or angry don't let the other side see this or hear this.   It is a sign of weakness and the other side will feed off of this misplaced emotion.

8)   **Note taker's role** - We cannot listen, think ahead and write with great accuracy in a fast moving big budget, conference call, negotiation.   This is where pulling in a note taker for the call pays off "big time". The detail a note taker can pick up is so valuable.   If the note taker is a colleague or superior…all the better because a person at this level can also slip you notes or questions you might not have been able to get to.

9)   **Close positively, with broad agreement** - Once you have closed out on all of the germane items on everyone's negotiation wish list, sign off the call positively and quit talking.   One misplaced word at this point of the proceeding could reopen the negotiation.   Stop. Sign off and get working.

10)   **We control the agreement language** - The last piece of any Mobile, Skype or e-Mail negotiation is the detail in the contract.   We always want to be the author of the contract if possible.   It is almost impossible to get every detail in a negotiation covered in a call.   Be alert. Control this part of the negotiation as there will always be little details that we would prefer to craft in the contract to benefit both sides while limiting exposure to our side.

Limit the number of potential land mines and trap doors in Mobile, Skype or e-Mail negotiations.   This is what top tier professional negotiators do naturally. See the negotiation from end to end before you get on the call and expect the unexpected.   Be proactive and above all manage risk in a constructive manner.

40

NEGOTIATION TIPS FOR WOMEN IN BUSINESS

I've been blessed with two heroes in life. Both are women. Jean, my mom had to finish high school and start a new life at age 39 when my dad suddenly died. Mom cried many a night coping with being forced back to high school to learn how to be a stenographer. With grit she dove into the foreign world of corporate business. Barbara, my sister sustained life changing injuries in a car accident that left her life hanging by a thread. She survived. In her early 30's, she also had to start all over again. Barb too went back to high school and then on to college where she completed a Diploma in Journalism. These women showed courage and tenacity beyond belief. They taught me that anything is possible if you remain flexible and just keep moving forward.

Business negotiation really does not have any set rules owing to the constant change in market conditions, civility and broadening cultural norms. This makes negotiation a platform of shifting sands on the best of days for professionals of all stripes and gender. For women who were brought up in a business environment it is a little easier to see. For women who have not had the benefit of growing up in a business environment, it is just another layer of challenge.

The tips I offer women in business are to help you see more clearly and stand firmly on the shifting sands of negotiation. They are designed to let you know you are not alone as you piece together the puzzle that business negotiation offers all who engage this unique business skill. Please take special note of the following:

1)   **Zebra camouflage** - Zebras are a brilliant wildlife design. They are strong, fast, intelligent and gifted with camouflage shading. Their black and white stripes that make them appear to blend in with their grassy surroundings. When they move on mass they look so similar it is hard for those pursuing them to separate them. If you are heading into a business negotiation environment where businessmen dress a certain way using certain colors or tones, mimic them. Do not be a giraffe among zebras. It is too easy to be singled out. If they are wearing corporate black or blue suits, I recommend you do the same. Act like a zebra. Be conservative to the point that you look the same as them in a business uniform. If you want to accent with color go with power colors. United States President Barrack Obama has been wearing purple ties of late. Billionaire businessman Donald Trump wears red ties regularly. These accent colors are power colors. I also like the color green with a blue suit. It speaks to creativity.

2)   **Detail** - One way to neutralize the other side and even doubters on our own negotiation team is to wow them with detail. Over prepare for a business negotiation. If you can un-script in the middle of a business negotiation because of your professional level of advanced detail and preparation, the other side will take notice.   All sides will give you greater respect.

3)   **Speaking their language** - As a business person who specialized in selling to and negotiating with large multi-market retail accounts, I cannot tell you how important is was to be able to speak their "retail language". I studied under two truly dedicated senior managers in the newspaper business. Both of these managers in previous business lives were executive managers in the retail business. Their lessons were simple. If you want to succeed at the negotiation table with top flight retailers, you had better be able to think like them, talk like them and add value to their world.   Otherwise, you are just another "suit" selling stuff.

4)   **Creative solutions** - There is no better way to level a playing field when you say *"I have studied your business. I see your pain. I have great ideas to help you"*. Large customers do not have the time they used to….to be more creative. They need suppliers who know their business and think ahead to anticipate their needs. This also means arriving at the bargaining table with a variety of ideas and BATNA options. Suppliers that master this advanced thinking will move up the client food chain and gain more opportunities on a first call basis.

5)   **Increasing negotiation strategies** - If you only have one or two "go to" business negotiation strategies you are vulnerable at the bargaining table. Professional buyers and sellers alike will identify your negotiation strategies and will work to neutralize them.   Read about business negotiation. Seek out webinars. Take courses in business negotiation. Educate yourself.   The more negotiation strategies you have at your disposal, the more often you will "make and save money" at the bargaining table.   Think of it this way.   If you lost 2% in every negotiation you entered in a single year, how would this affect your performance bonus?

6)   **Believing in yourself**   - Practice being your own best friend.   If you saw your best girlfriend berating herself over something that was just bad timing, random or out of her control…what would you say to comfort her? You'd be inclined to talk to her about her strengths and accomplishments.   If you truly believe in yourself you will *"participate in positive self-talk"* as noted author Lucinda Bassett often says.   Tell yourself "you are smart, bright, dedicated and professional".   I know what my heroes would do.

PART V - THE CLOSE

41

MANAGING RISK

There is almost always risk in sales negotiations. The question is whether it is negative risk or positive risk. If there is no risk in a negotiation then we are all just buying and selling products and services at market rates or at rates with unknown mark-ups.

The breadth of risk tends to follow factors such as the cost, quality, complexity, scarcity and time sensitivity of a product/service. Depending on the product/service and where it is produced there are other risks to acknowledge and calculate.

Professional business negotiators do their best to mitigate and manage risk. Here are a few examples of how they do it:

1)   **Start homework early** - Very simply…money is lost at the bargaining table when the homework for the negotiation is compressed into a short period of time. Professionals, if they have an option will always take the time to know as much as they can to improve their odds of closing a smart deal. It sounds cliché like but time in this case really does translate into money.

2)   **Understand everyone's economic situation** - Can you imagine if you knew the party you were negotiating with was anticipating a labor problem? What about if they were faced with a scarcity of a key component of their product causing potential for a production quality problem?   Would all of this economic information affect your management of risk in the negotiations?   You betcha.

3)   **Understand needs of other side** - What if you knew prior to reaching the bargaining table that the other side needed to close a deal with you to hit their quarterly or year-end sales targets?   How would this affect your approach to cost modeling with them? In a word, lots.

4)   **Research competitive pricing** - This might sound academic but too often long relationship, negotiation partners just become comfortable while competitive market prices are edging lower.   Conversely, scarcity owing to unforeseen natural catastrophe can drive prices up.   Think drought and flooding in this case.

5)   **Goal pricing and walk away** - The gap between goal pricing and walking away from a deal is called "the bargaining continuum (AKA ZOPA)".   This gap exists for both negotiation parties and sets up a unique dance.   Both bargaining parties will make their business case for what final pricing should be.   The party who best understands their cost modeling will have a better chance of mitigating risk.

6)   **Opening and closing negotiation positions** - Recently, I asked a seasoned mergers and acquisitions (M&A) specialist his preference for opening with a price or waiting for the other side to start.   He firmly stated he liked to see what price the other side wanted and then his side would counter.   He was convinced over a long period of many M&A deals that on average the party that started the negotiation got the worst of it.

By comparison, my experience in the negotiating many large media contracts is that the party with the best cost modeling and best reconnaissance who stated price first usually got the best of the deal. This reduced risk.   We must conclude that knowing your industry and negotiation partner is essential to mitigating risk.

7)   **Control content of deal** - When closing out on a negotiation make sure your side drafts the content of the contract. This allows you to control and interpret the language in the contract, to a degree. It also allows your side to arrange the order of the items and special side bars of the deal.   If the other side does not like

your interpretation of the deal they will simply cross out what they don't like write in their changes and the deal closes.   If not, the deal stands with your   content.

Professional business negotiators always manage risk wherever they can.

42

POWERFUL SCRIPTING AND UN-SCRIPTING

In a buyer's role, one of the first things I try to do is knock the seller off his/her presentation script in a negotiation. This makes the seller vulnerable to questions they did not prepare for and opens up so many opportunities for the buyer to save lots of money.

When I was a seller, I can't tell you how many times a tricky or impatient buyer would leap ahead of my prepared remarks or during presentation of materials. The buyer would begin asking questions about my research or proposal figures completely out of the order or context that I had intended to present them.

Physically and mentally scripting yourself for large or important negotiations has a number of crucial functions and benefits:

1)   **Strategy and objectives** - Engaging in an important sales negotiation without a solid game plan will weaken our ability to solidly deliver on our negotiation objectives. In large or important sales negotiations we must arrive at the bargaining table with confidence and the agility to counter unexpected moves from the other side.

2)   **Creating order** - When participating in a sales negotiation with many moving parts and complex issues it is important to have a vision. How are we planning to bring this information into a flow that best reflects our goals and objectives? Ranking and weighting key dollar value issues is important. Creating a flow for our presentation of the facts and arguments is the art in the deal. Flow urges us to present information in a manner that gets our points across without making the other side feel uncomfortable. Finally, this mental mapping of negotiation issues gives us a view of a finished picture or forward vision of a completed negotiation.

3)   **Preparing for objections** - If we are able to articulate our objectives, there is an equal need to visualizing the objectives from the other side. These two sets of objectives will reveal points of mutual interest and points where an expectation gap is evident. The expectation gap generates debate and sometimes objections. By preparing to listen to the other side and empathize with their objections we can create an environment where we can educate the other side on the value our proposal offerings. This helps define our unique point of difference in the market. If objections are handled professionally with good closure it may actually offer an opportunity to ask for the deal.

4)   **Enthusiasm, conviction and momentum** - Enthusiasm and conviction are inner feelings. No one can teach us how to be enthusiastic. If we are well prepared and enthusiastic about our position in a business negotiation, this builds momentum.   In a negotiation, if the other side senses you are legitimately confident, they will take notice. They give you credit for your preparation and will be comforted by our honest conviction.   By lowering the anxiety of our negotiation partner we may actually draw them closer to our objectives and get a smart deal done.

5)   **Script to safely un-script** - Olympic and professional athletes prepare for weeks, months and sometimes years for a single competitive performance. This preparation strengthens their endurance and creates much needed muscle memory. It also frees them from having too many things to think about when they execute complex movements at high speed.   Their goal is to visualize the routine and have a couple of key thoughts. They feel the routine without actually doing it. It's called "getting in the zone".

A version of the same thing happens with large or important business negotiations. If we have examined all important research, objectives, goals, arithmetic and foreseeable outcomes it prepares us to let these factors rest in our minds as a few key thoughts. This deep scripting allows us to safely un-script and not worry about the unexpected. It allows us to totally focus on our negotiation partner and the feel of the negotiation venue. We zero in on the physical and emotion state of our negotiation partner. We are so prepared; we are living in the present. We are "in the zone" to think and act creatively. This helps us recognize a buying signal and close out on a smart and fulfilling deal for both parties.

So remember, scripting and un-scripting in a business negotiation can help you make or save money. You just have to be prepared to recognize the opportunity.

43

CREDIBILITY AT THE NEGOTIATION TABLE PAYS

Credibility at the negotiation table pays big time. Having participated in many multi-million dollar negotiations, I can tell you for certain I always ramped up my negotiation arsenal to equal or surpass my negotiation partner. I did this partly for economic reasons. I did this partly for future encounters with these same individuals and their respective business colleagues.

When readying for a large negotiation, I am always looking for an edge at the negotiation table. Below is a partial list of negotiation essentials that will help you with bargaining credibility. It will add to your potential to "make and save money" in the process:

1)   **Preparation** - If you are not totally prepared for a big money negotiation you should be not be surprised if you get skinned. Enough said.

2)   **Reputation** - Your industry reputation as a skilled negotiator is like having an invisible partner in the room with you. It can be an intimidation factor for the other side. It means they have to look at your past negotiation performances and try to uncover a trend. This helps them possibly anticipate your

future decision making process. It means, our negotiation partner must maximize preparation or suffer the consequences. It can impart a sense of positive risk for our side. The industry should not be surprised if we bring new innovative thinking to the bargaining table. Reputation means, we can shift tactical and strategic gears more freely.

3)   **Table presence** - I have played a lot of "Texas No Limit Poker". The first thing you want to do when you play the first half hour at a poker table is to get the other participants to believe that you are either playing tight, loose, creatively, recklessly or tactically. You choose the table presence/image that gives you that maximum amount of flexibility to shift gears in the game if you need to. It helps our side reap rewards for playing a particular role that might be similar to or contrary to that of the general population of the table. The same holds true at a big negotiation table. We want to be seen in a certain way. We want the other side to feel a certain way in response to our presence. These actions give us latitude to shape time at the table. The person who has the most influence on time compression or decompression at a negotiation table is in a powerful position. Table presence can also be altered by the way we dress. Remember, if your negotiation partner's team looks and runs like a herd of zebras, we want to blend in. Presence can be altered by our physical and emotional being. Do we look tired, stressed or concerned? Are we chatty or are we quiet? Or, best of all, do we exude a wonderful sense of inner peace and confidence. Always think about the table presence you are emitting at a negotiation session because your negotiation partner is taking notice. They are evaluating their chances of advancing their objectives based on your capability and or susceptibility.

4)   **Focus** - Liberating your mind to live in the present is a tremendous advantage at a bargaining table. Your singular focus means you are firing on all cylinders. It means your analytics skills are peaking. It means, you have the clarity to realize when it is profitable to close a deal. It puts you in a position to advance positive risk and mitigate negative risk while still striving for a smart deal that maintains our productive relationship with our negotiation partner. Factors that inhibit focus are a lack of preparation, fatigue, stress and fear of failure.

5)   **Creativity** - Free flowing, 360 degree thought production in the heat of a negotiation is absolutely powerful. To our negotiation partner it means that we are open to expanding perimeters or reducing boundaries to get a deal done. It also shows the other side that if we are creative while closing pressure deals that

we could also be counted on to think similarly when solving important customer problems. Watching someone channel and harness creative thinking is a thing of beauty. There are many bright managers in business who show great talent in leading teams. They are not all necessarily creative thinkers. When you are in the presence of a great creative thinker in a negotiation, drink up the experience with all of your senses. Ask yourself…how did they just do that? What was the spark that ignited that creative combustion? Who does this person model themselves after? Where did they learn this lateral style of thinking? What is their source of creative inspiration? Which negotiation learning programs have they completed? How do I learn from this great experience and weave this creative moment into my next important business negotiation?

As you prepare for your next big money negotiation, plan, visualize how you are going to display your table image and negotiation credibility. In preparation think creativity and calm assertiveness. Rest well the day before the face to face negotiation. Compress all important negotiation information including your BATNA into mental crystals. Build and continue to reinforce your reputation as a savvy, professional, business negotiator.

44

EFFECTIVE TRIAL CLOSES

At a gathering, I asked a relative in my wife's family who once owned a large car dealership what the best piece of negotiation advice he had received over his storied career. He took his time to respond and said "yes I remember it well. A giant in the auto industry once told me that to be successful in car sales/negotiations, I had to visualize that I was always standing in a round room." He had passed along a gem that remains with me today and a quote that I often use in our Centroid Training sessions. Metaphorically, he was saying take the corners out of the room so you have room to back up and regroup.

One of the themes I like to leave our Centroid Training graduates with is that nicely crafted questions delivered politely are innocuous. We can ask tons of carefully crafted questions in our pursuit of a "yes". An example of a Trial Close question is "What would it take to get this deal done?"

The alternative is to ask a question in a hard, closed ended fashion. An example of a closed question is…. "Do we have a deal?" This small question might seem like a risk free question in a business negotiation but, it isn't. By asking this direct question we have initiated a "coin toss" result. The answer will ultimately lead to a "yes or no". This means, by questioning in this direct manner I've opened up a 50% chance of a "no" in the overarching negotiation. I have inadvertently backed myself into a corner by asking this question so directly.

Back to visualizing we are operating in a round room in a negotiation. By asking a direct question, I have senselessly built a corner where there was none. I am boxing myself in. Question? Is there an appropriate time to directly ask for the deal? Yes there is. The time to directly ask for the deal is when you have exhausted all lower risk questions and or when you are running out of time.

The Trial Close example above sounds very similar to a "high value" question. High value questions are questions that begin with specific words such as; "Who, Where, When, Which, Where and How". So what is the difference between a high value question and a Trial Close? The answer is it has to do with tightening the scope of our query toward the end of a bargaining session. Trial Close questions are used to surgically expose blockages or impediments to the deal closing. Trial Closes are also used to trigger spontaneous closure by the customer. Trial close questions also tend to steer toward opportunities in Timing, Place, Utility, Profitability, Success, Approval and Authority. Questions that look like this:

1)   Where would you like to begin our proposal?

2)   When is the best time to initiate this proposal?

3)   What about this proposal do you like and which of your stakeholders would like it too?

4)   Which group in your organization would benefit most from our proposal?

5)   How do you visualize closing out this deal?

Trial Closes are a thing of beauty because they do all of the heavy lifting a Direct Close does without boxing us in. And, if you are in collaboration mode with your customer, the customer may actually offer up valuable information. In a better case scenario, they actually share creative approaches they have on the potential deal and start to sell us on their ideas to get final closure of the deal. In the best case scenario, they may even say "You know we've really discussed the opportunities and exposed the risk in this proposal. I think there are more positives than negatives. Let's sign this deal and get going."

Centroid Training participants learn that Trial Close questions are money questions and I sincerely believe this. When heading into an important negotiation rank your Trial Close Questions for dollar value and effect. Think about how much time you have in large account negotiations with senior executive buyers? The answer is, not much. So, craft your trial close questions carefully. Rank them. Practice them. Role play with them. The better you get at delivering Trial Close questions in pressure cooker negotiations, the more deals you will close with the lowest amount of risk.

45

WIN MORE WITH VALUE STATEMENTS

Most sales negotiations sail smoothly largely because two parties have found enough common ground to take time to listen to each other's needs and aspirations. Most customers do extensive homework on their suppliers to mitigate risk and to understand the suppliers' point of difference or unique vertical within their business category.

If all goes well, both parties carefully explain their objectives within their needs. Generally, an expectation gap is identified by both bargaining parties. Some kind of give and take commences to bring about amicable closure of a deal.

In tougher negotiations savvy customers will do their best to knock sellers off their script and throw out creative objections. Armor piercing queries appear to double check their known facts and back check our claims. Seasoned sales negotiators expect to be put to the test and are prepared to answer "burden of proof questions". It's just part of the process.

Patrick Tinney

Most sellers have been trained to handle a wide variety of objections from customers. If they handle these objections constructively then the negotiation just gets back on course and the deal closes out with a solid Win/win agreement.

In spite of all of the above, some negotiations just get bogged down in objections that are not fully satisfied with available answers to them. Somehow elements of doubt enter the discussion and bargaining stalls. So how does this happen? Typically, there is a missing step – the value statement.

Value statements are a bridge between the skillful handling of a customer objection and a trial close. Value statements are an overarching truth about a seller's position in their business category that helps solidify their position for longer term relationships with larger customers.

Value statements are designed to help reassure a customer the experience they will have with our product or service has been enjoyed by many of the customer's contemporaries. These experiences are constructive and accretive.

Value statements acknowledging a customer concern/objection sound like this:

1) *"The reason our large customers purchase our products year after year is <u>because</u> our delivery and post-delivery follow-up is second to none."*

2) *"The reason we get so many product trials with our large customers is <u>because</u> we vigorously back test the products to mitigate negative risk."*

3) *"The reason our large customers come to us first with problems or opportunities is <u>because</u> they know we have a great creative team working tirelessly to create unique solutions for unique customers."*

So as we see from the above examples value statements are "truth and positive affirmation <u>because</u> statements". Value statements are the bridge between skillfully handled customers objections and masterful trial close questions. Value statements put the customer at ease knowing that the seller and her company stand behind their promises and have lived their brand. Value statements are an affirmation of the reliable repeatable promises your company stands for.

So be smart. Incorporate value statements into your next negotiation when the going gets tough. Your customers will appreciate that you are listening to them and that you and your company care.

Remember, large customers not only want great negotiated deals, they want to know that your company will show up and live up to its promises rain or shine.

46

SMARTLY NAVIGATE PRICE TRAPS

Recently, I read a column on business negotiation that suggested one of the ways to navigate the buyer price tactic… "You are too expensive"…was to simply shrink the quantity of the seller's offering to fit the buyer's price. Is this a bad idea? Not really. The challenge is that price is so much more complicated than the option of a "scale to fit" equation.

Price is also about quality, time, brand, uniqueness, demand, supply, risk, innovation competition and hidden value. If you are able to ask the right questions of potential buyers prior to and during negotiations using the above topics in the right combinations you will be much more successful at navigating price traps. You will also be much clearer about the buyer's true objectives and intentions toward you and your company.

So let's explore tips and topics to navigate price traps in negotiations:

1)   **Quality** - The overall quality of our offering is key, relative to price. If quality can be adjusted then price definitely has the potential to be adjusted up or down.

2)   **Time** - If we can alter the timelines to deliver our offering then it is very likely that price can be altered.   I once told a printer that his company could print our products on off-shifts to help him better manage his production time schedule. I just wanted good quality at a great price.   We both got what we wanted.

3)   **Brand** - To some buyers brand means nothing.   To others it is paramount. Understanding your brand and its positioning in the market has a huge bearing on price.   Try not to get too caught up in all of the noisy definitions of brand.   The clearest meaning of brand is…."What are our consistent, repeatable, promises that the market expects us to execute flawlessly?"   When you can articulate your brand promises effortlessly, you will speak clearly to the market and avoid unnecessary price traps.

4)   **Uniqueness** - This is just a pretty way to describe our "Point of Difference". If we can confidently describe our point of difference the negative price discussion stands a much greater chance of being neutralized.

5)   **Demand** - Markets of all types are driven by need and demand.   If there is great demand in the market, expect prices to rise.   In everyday life, think of the lack of fresh drinking water in many parts of Africa and the Middle East. At the opposite end of the spectrum, think of asbestos.   Who uses asbestos products anymore?

6)   **Supply** - The overall availability of our product in the market has a great bearing on price.   If our product is scarce and in demand, prices may go up. Think Apple Mobile products.   If however, there are too many sellers in the market of our product and not enough buyers, think commoditization and lower prices.

7)   **Risk** - Most businesses do their best to manage and control risk.   Upside risk exposure usually demands insurance or higher prices.   Risk off environments where there is little monetary exposure generally ushers in lower prices.   To illustrate, when hurricane season is on in the USA there is always a chance that oil exploration rigs in the Gulf of Mexico could be damaged when these huge storms erupt.   If storms are tracking toward oil exploration rigs at harrowing speeds, expect the market to price in upside risk and higher prices for oil.

8)   **Innovation** - Buyers love creative ideas.   Businesses readily buy innovation that puts them ahead of their competitors, even for a short period of

time. If your company thinks innovation when it develops and markets its products, it can ask for higher prices in an otherwise stagnant market.

9) **Competition** - The marketplace loves and depends on competition to keep negotiated prices in check. If however, you develop a product with unique expertise required to operate it you can demand remarkably high prices. Not so long ago there was no such thing as a website. Most companies just used traditional media such as print and broadcast to speak to their customers. When the first websites were introduced to the market, financial institutions in the western world instantly realized e-commerce potential and spent enormous amounts of money getting their brands up on the internet. In those days, there were very few technology companies who had the knowledge to write complicated code to power websites. A quorum of unique internet development companies with great programming and database manipulation expertise created a sellers vertical market. These website wizards regularly tested just how much the market would bear for the build out of websites. It was a technology banquet. Sellers ruled negotiations and pricing.

10) **Hidden value** - Many businesses have purchased equipment, buildings, licenses, technology and data that are fully paid for. In a negotiation where price is at the fore, many of the above items may be of great interest to your negotiation partner and therefore neutralize the importance of price. Again, you have to ask the right questions to navigate price traps in business negotiations.

47

IDENTIFYING AND NAVIGATING AN IMPASSE

An impasse tells us the structural nature of a proposal is perceived as being flawed, lopsided or undoable by one or both parties in a negotiation. It could be a deadlock on price, time, quality, service or other factors. If we dig past the intellectual side of the discussion, the impasse has strong emotional underpinnings.

When we reach an impasse in a negotiation with a customer we could be thinking any of the following:

1)   Why can't you see my side?

2)   You just don't get it.

3)   You are taking advantage of our relationship.

4)   You are hiding something.

5)   I no longer trust you and I am fearful of your intentions.

6)   Can we find someone else to replace this business partner?

7)   Can we just walk away from this business partner?

Pretty ugly. This is more common than you think especially in a stagnant or deflationary economy. Not only do we have the above emotional side of the discussion but, we also have the tactical side of how it all happened. Don't rule out negotiator egos running amuck.

In its most rudimentary form, a negotiation impasse is telling the bargaining participants that they are no longer in their "comfort zone" to get a deal done. At Centroid Training we call the comfort zone "The Bargaining Continuum".

When we are in the Bargaining Continuum (AKA ZOPA) there is hope that an opportunity will arise to engage in bargaining reciprocity to close a smart and fulfilling deal for both parties.

It's impractical to think your company will be able to avoid negotiation impasses with business partners. Here are some tips that will help your company navigate better positions to lessen the likelihood of an impasse in negotiation.

Conduct reconnaissance on your negotiation partner's world. Gain as much intelligence on them as you can. By understanding more about their business, and their future, your company stands a much better chance of signing smart, sustainable deals.

Rank and weigh objectives for your company and theirs. Next understand their objectives and know what they really want combined with the clarity of what you really want. This knowledge will have greater opportunity to pull the other side closer to you. This action will help close the expectation gap that comes with all negotiations. This process lowers negative risk.

The spirit of the deal. We must learn to listen and have appreciation for the other side, even when we'd rather not. No empathy?? Sorry, not likely to get a sustainable deal done.

Be realistic with cost demands. If you are low balling or hard balling, what do you expect the other side to do? How can we honestly expect to lower our costs by raising our negotiation partner's costs? Creative soft cost proposals from our side will add value for them. This may help offset some costs for the other side.

Make your proposals simple, understandable and accessible. If your negotiation partner cannot clearly understand the details and benefits of your proposal it will only slow the negotiation down. And, yes, you guessed it, start the ball rolling toward an impasse.

Have a backup plan. Have several back up plans if you like. You can say "no" politely as often as you like in a business negotiation and generally not offend the other side. Just be careful not to say "no never". Remember never is a long, long time and leaves you no outs.

Most negotiation impasses are avoidable. The key is having a negotiation thought process that works to lower relationship risk while still trying to get smart deals done.

PART VI - THE AFTERMATH

48

THE VALUE OF POST MORTEM IN NEGOTIATIONS

All great sales negotiation professionals look to their victories and stinging loses for inspiration for future bargaining engagements. A post mortem of any business negotiation will always reveal a treasure trove of new and valuable information.

Negotiation professionals immediately prepare for the next negotiation with regular business partners by capturing every detail of the negotiation they have just finished.   They make copious notes on all topics within the negotiation. Seasoned negotiators may take weeks to discreetly probe their negotiation partners to garner even more information and to draw final conclusions on how they will prepare for and execute their next negotiation engagement.   The short line is "learn from your mistakes".

Negotiation professionals go to these great lengths because like great chess masters each opponent they engage has a specific line of thought as they lay out their negotiation plans.   Our negotiation partner's logic base may repeat itself. For example, they may choose a specific time of day to meet to enhance their access to information.   They may like to meet in the morning when they are most uncluttered mentally and most refreshed from a good sleep.   They may also choose a specific style of venue to create a mood such as austerity, collaboration, conciliation or they may just have need for quick fulfilling closure.

There is a lot to think about and process when big money negotiations are in play. I'm known to ask clients this question. "What if I could help you realize a 1% gain on every business negotiation you complete on an annualized basis, what would this mean to your business?" It is one of those client queries that makes a very small number grow into a very large and intriguing number.

Below are four topics and questions to add to your next business negotiation post mortem:

1)   **Their objectives** - Did we do our best job unearthing their true objective and motives? In my experience, most business negotiation partners are pretty forthcoming and transparent about what they want simply because they are trying to foster an environment of trust. Many times this mindset can lead to collaboration in bargaining, which is surely the gold standard in business negotiation. Over the years however, there have been a few negotiation partners that say one thing and play us to the hilt to get what they truly wanted in a manner that might be construed as feckless and reckless. We always have to ask ourselves, did we really guide them into the bargaining continuum or were we duped?

2)   **Tactics they used** - I love the game of tactics in a business negotiation because it is where some of the fine art in bargaining is displayed. Tactics are what we see, hear, smell and feel. Can we identify each tactic and catalogue it for the next time with a frequent bargaining partner with an appropriate neutralizer from our side? What verbal expressions did they use? What body language did they recoil into? What did they do to move us off of our script in the heat of the moment? Was there a physical tell when they were getting close to their objectives?

3)   **Strategies they used** - The difference between novice and seasoned negotiators is the strategies they employ. A novice negotiator may only have a couple of go to strategies they implement under a wide variety of situations with varied success. Whereas, a seasoned negotiator shifts gears with a catalogue of effective strategies like a formula one racecar driver who adapts to the terrain of a high speed track.   If you can identify your negotiation partner's strategies you

have a huge advantage in guiding the other side toward your business negotiation objectives.

4)   **Improvements we must make** - The old saying "fool me once shame on you.   Fool me twice shame on me"…applies.   In order to become the best business negotiator you can you have to continually pull even your finest bargaining efforts apart to look for further improvement. Educate yourself to recognize when a trusted negotiation partner is offering you an opening to complete a great innovative deal. Think more about end to end negotiation strategies.   Understand the importance of your negotiation partner's business culture.   Think collaboration.   Look for the good in business partners and conclude smart deals that stand the test of time. Remember, great skill sets take years of practice and refinement.   Start your business negotiation post mortem rituals today and begin to make and save more money.

PART VII - 12 NEGOTIATION STRATEGIES

12 Buyer Negotiation Strategies
Sellers Need To Know

"On a good day, business negotiation is 100 shades of grey." – Patrick Tinney

As we noted earlier in *Unlocking Yes,* most business people vastly overestimate their negotiation skills. Over the years, I have asked hundreds and hundreds of sales and procurement executives how they score themselves as business negotiators. Inevitably, the majority rank their proficiency as 6.5 to 7.5 on a scale of 1 to 10. When asked to name their top three negotiation strategies and how they implement them, they usually turn red in the face or just stand there, stunned. Unable to name a single negotiation strategy, is a huge disconnect in either a buyer or seller profession.

Our goal in this section of *Unlocking Yes* is to help you identify, name, and associate seller and time compression risk for 12 negotiation strategies that buyers use. By understanding these strategies, you as a seller will have a greater opportunity to react quicker to strategy. This allows you to weigh your options, neutralize the strategy, or call for a change in strategy to maximize your negotiation potential.

At Centroid Training, we love to teach negotiation strategy. These are 12 of our favorites we see being used on sellers over and over again. Any one of these strategies can be used by buyers singularly or in combination. When used in combination, these negotiation strategies become extra powerful. Sellers beware.

1.   Buyer Creates a Bidding War, With an Account Review

This is a strong buyer negotiation strategy.   It puts absolutely all sellers on notice that there is a tectonic move happening.   The buyer risk is reasonably low with this negotiation strategy.   However, if the buyer changes top suppliers, there is always a window of transition.   Changes of systems is where big problems can and often do occur.   Seller risk though is very high. This is when your navigational and allied relationships throughout the buyer company will be tested. It is a time to contact people throughout the buyer's organization to find out what you as a seller can do to save the account. What is causing this account review? From a time compression point of view you are on an hour glass clock.   Every minute you do not act to save the account and identify the event that brought about the account review, your risk meter moves up.

Tip: If all else fails have your company President directly call the buyer President.   Chief Executives generally have a collegial approach to speaking directly to hidden, often game-changing issues.

2.   Buyer Sells Concept of Yes…Will You Take This Price?

The "concept of yes at this price" buyer negotiation strategy is brilliant because the buyer is assuming the role of a seller.   The buyer, however, still holds the purse strings on the deal making this strategy a stinger.   The risk for the buyer is very low.   The risk for the seller is very high.

The concept of yes is all about compressing the seller's time without the seller being fully aware.   In our buyer's market, we experience this strategy as a mainstay for crafty buyers who don't care about fostering close relationships. The seller has to be nimble with profit margins and hidden customer value to manage this buyer strategy.   The seller also has to be mindful of the full array of pricing they have offered their entire customer base for fear of a price contagion.   The "concept of yes at this price" strategy has no limit on account size.   I know of one case where a large advertiser used it on a daily newspaper.   So, it can be used in large volume negotiations if both buyer and seller are acutely aware of competitive pricing and cost structures.

Tip: If you research your customers well, you can pick off the type of client who will use the concept of yes. Be sure to have easy access to your client files or pricing channel you offer them at all times. Request a relaxation of time to do the buyer's offer justice. Be creative with your back-up plans. Be careful to limit the duration of a deal you cannot live with over the long haul. Remember, where pricing is concerned, everything leaks.

3.   Buyer Creates a Share & Compare Quote Scheme

Share & Compare is perhaps my least favorite buy strategy. It is a blunt instrument used by aggressive negotiators who generally place little value on confidentiality and long-term relationships. The risk for the buyer is low in this environment with the exception of one key area – trust. How can a seller trust a buyer who is using another seller's confidential proposal as a leverage instrument? The risk to the seller is elevated in that closing a deal with a buyer using this strategy means that our seller proposal/deal is now expected to be public knowledge in the foreseeable future. Time compression is reasonably high. The seller will have to make a decision fairly quickly as to whether they want to pursue this business knowing the buyer could be using the same strategy with several of our competitors simultaneously.

This strategy is a mugs game. And, believe it or not, it has been used by large dollar volume buyers when they felt they needed to leverage a negotiation.

Tip: Visualize working with this customer several years ahead. What does the relationship look like in your mind? How much valuable information can we reasonably pass over to this customer? Do we take them our best ideas? Do we treat this relationship as a commoditized strategic sell?

My counsel is to be very "Spartan" with releasing deep data to a customer that utilizes "Share & Compare." Know that you are basically buying the business with this customer. Be prepared for volatility in maintaining this sale/negotiation as it will always be on the auction block.

4.   Buyer Requests Test Rate Scheme

Test or Pilot rates really do have a place in Win/Win negotiations.   If both sides are sincere in their exploration of a product trial, building a long-term and a trusting relationship, then test rates are a great place to start.

Some buyers just use the test rate discussion as a window to understand the seller's profitability and lay the groundwork for a discussion around the test rate becoming a permanent rate.   The thinking from the buyer's side is that if you can afford to run a test rate that this must be close to your profit line.   If the buyer starts to understand your profit margins then, the carrot discussion will begin.   And the next question will be, "How about a large contract at this test rate?"

This strategy puts great pressure and risk on the seller.   The buyer is under some risk, but, always has the option of cancelling the contract if no penalty clauses are spelled out in a signed contract.   Time compression risk can be quite wide with this strategy as the buyer often ends up selling the strategy to the seller.

Tip: As a seller, test or pilot rates really are a great tool in a negotiation for a trial. The problem is that once introduced to the market, pricing is a hard thing to control.   To quote an old colleague of mine, "everything leaks".   So we have to be very careful with price contagion, especially when dealing with large accounts. The other concern is if the test account really grows dramatically, what does this do to the overall profitability of your seller business?   There is nothing worse than having one gigantic account and no profit.

So when we are heading into a test or pilot program, I recommend putting a time or inventory limit on it. We then blend up the test rate with a proposal that turns the test rate into normalized pricing consistent with your industry.

5.   The Secondary Target Strategy

The secondary target strategy is a common strategy that many business people get tricked by.   A former 10 million dollar newspaper customer of mine used to play this secondary strategy like a violin in our large annual contract negotiations.

He would only negotiate on the primary lines of our business and with total ferocity.   If we introduced the secondary lines into the negotiation, he would tell us that "we will get to it in due time." He would drag the primary line negotiation on for days, even weeks, grinding out details on this product line and then finally acquiesce, telling us he was tired with the whole discussion. Then he would grumble to himself that he had been taken again.

On the secondary product line he would tell our sales team because we had taken advantage of him so badly on the primary line, there would be no discussion on the secondary line. He said, "Rates must stay flat with the secondary line. No more discussion. Don't even think about it."

Guess what? Our customer's whole strategy was to keep the secondary product rates low. He was slowly scaling back on the primary line and was prepared to let rates rise a little on a diminishing primary line base. Brilliant.

Tip: It takes courage, but we all have to be prepared to ask armor-piercing questions when we enter any negotiation to separate fact from assumptions. We have to ask questions to remove blocker tactics and cut away false information. We must trust our negotiation partners, but we must also verify their deepest and true intentions. Once you have verified the customer's intention, you can bring the negotiation back into its proper balance to create value for both negotiation partners.

6.   **Split the Difference Strategy**

The "Split the Difference Strategy" is one of the most overused and most misunderstood negotiation strategies I can think of. There are entire business categories (think Real Estate) that use this negotiation strategy as a foundation. Therefore, as an outsider, if you don't want to play split the difference you are in many cases considered rude or uneducated. This last notion is anything but the truth.

The problem with "Split the Difference" is that it usually benefits the negotiation partner initiating the strategy. Therefore, the risk is laid on the party receiving this negotiation strategy. One more thing, time compression risk can be a big factor. Let me explain. Let's say you see a house for sale at $200,000 and you have a mortgage approval for exactly $180,000. You put an offer of $180,000 thinking the price you are offering is fair after reviewing the house prices in the neighborhood and the condition of the home. The seller wanting to sell at full price says, "I will sell to you if we can split the difference in our valuations". If you accept this offer, the seller has convinced you to raise your bid by $10,000 or approximately 6% over what you thought was fair value for the house. My question is…why would anyone go into a negotiation knowing that they will be expected, even cajoled to raise their offer just to appear civil or in good form? Since we have no opportunity to raise more money asking for chattels in the home is pointless.

Tip: If you are negotiating with someone and they say "come on, let's just split the difference," ask yourself, why would this negotiation partner want to do this? Who has the advantage in this scheme? Smart money says go back and look at your BATNA, if the numbers don't make sense go to your next BATNA or politely refuse the kind offer.

7.   The Buyer Creates A Performance-Based Scheme

Performance payment schemes are not new. I don't even think they are bad as a negotiation strategy. All of the risk however, lies with the seller. Time compression is not really a factor, unless the buyer makes it so.

I remember meeting with a prospective client. I was showing him some of our Centroid Training Programs and there was a modicum of interest from the client's side. The client said, "We want this to be a performance-based payment to Centroid. We want some of your skin in the game." The client was pounding his point home. I wasn't getting paid until he was sure Centroid Training Programs had made him money.

My response was simple. I said, "Sure, I can live with a performance-based agreement. But let me understand what I am agreeing to. So…you want me to deliver a training program with no initial payment. This means, you want to use my money and then you decide later if you are going to pay me. I get this. You are demanding total transparency from me. So then, in the name of transparency you (Mr. Client) must be open to me reviewing your revenue intake by each salesperson I train. This would be the only fair way for me to confirm that our training improved your sales revenue. Am I correct in my understanding of your request?" The client looked at me and replied with a snarl "There is no_____ way you are ever looking at my revenue reports. Not a chance." I said, "Well (Mr. Client), it appears the performance payment negotiation strategy you proposed is not viable for either party. So, what is your back-up negotiation strategy?" He had not thought that far. You can only imagine how the proceedings went from there.

Tip: I do not recommend proceeding with any performance negotiation agreements unless there is total transparency and guarantee of payment upon proof of performance by the seller.

8.   The Rule Book Legitimacy Strategy

The rule book legitimacy strategy is used by both buyers and sellers in negotiations. As a seller, I would use a rule book to explain to clients the minimums of a product they had to buy, the sizes of products they had to buy and so on. In many cases, these rules were non-negotiable to maintain profit. Buyers use the rule book very well too. Some limit the amount of time a seller has to meet with them. Some will not allow you to go to dinner with them unless they pay their half. Some buyers issue RFP (long request for proposal) documents sent to sellers designed to unearth our profitability. In some cases, they even claim our intellectual property as their own once they've used it.

Here is an example of how the rule book has been used. Years ago, I bought a new car that I loved. It was a few months away from coming off of its five year extended warranty. I asked the dealership service advisor to put a note in my file to advise me a few weeks before the warranty ended and to call me to book the car in for its final service. The call never came. Just before I was heading off on a week's vacation I remembered that my warranty was running out that weekend. It also happened to be a national long weekend when businesses would be lighter on staff. It was about 3 p.m. on Friday afternoon, when I called the dealership to request an early appointment for the following day. If no appointment could be scheduled I would ask for a short extension on my warranty. Both requests were denied. There would be no mechanics working this weekend, and my warranty strictly stated that once the last day was over, the warranty was no longer valid. I then asked my representative to call the manufacturer directly on my behalf to plead my case. He didn't think that was possible but agreed to check. Time was ticking by and finally the answer was "no" again. I then went on to try several other approaches to reasonably solve the problem with the dealership over the phone and all conversations ending with a polite "no".

Finally, it dawned on me. The dealership was not working on my behalf. They were using their rule book to win the day. It was now about 4:30 p.m., and I jumped in my car and drove like blazes to the dealership. My service person was there at the service desk, and I told him I wanted my car serviced immediately and that it was under warranty. He looked at me like I was crazy and recounted all of our earlier conversations about what they could not do. I told him I didn't care. The fact that the dealership was poorly staffed was not my problem. I told him "my car warranty is valid and I want it serviced now." As a matter of fact, I told him to write a service order up and time-stamp it. We had reversed roles. I was using his rule book and hitting him with it. He was in shock. He walked into his manager's office and after a long conversation he came out and said they might be able to have someone look at my car. A gent appeared behind me in street clothing and said he was a mechanic just going off shift but, he would go for a test drive with me. The car sounded fine to him. The mechanic said "let's go back to the shop and quickly put it up on the hoist so I can see the undercarriage of your car." Right away he said, "Your transmission is leaking. This may be as simple as replacing a seal or it could be something larger." In the end, it was just a transmission seal. And, it was fixed under warranty at a later date owing to my persistence on having the work order dated and time stamped.

Tip: When confronted by a negotiation partner that is determined to use their rule book as a negotiation tool, make a point to ask for a copy of their rule book and study it. Study it hard. There are usually little holes in contracts that can be interpreted in different ways. And, if you are creative you can use their rule book to your advantage in a challenging negotiation. Make special note that the rule book legitimacy strategy is used regularly by large corporations and government agencies.

9.   Poor Mouth. "We Have No Money" Strategy

If I have heard poor mouth once I have heard, "We have no money", as a strategy a hundred times.   This strategy is not limited to small businesses that truly face day-to-day survival.   Just the opposite is true.   Truly successful mid-tier and even large corporations use the poor mouth strategy.   When larger businesses use this negotiation strategy it is premeditated, and it could be cultural.

Be wary of "C Level" officers of businesses who want to probe for information and ask for advice about their problems.   When you enquire about budget the violins will start to play in the back ground.   One CEO who ran a nationally branded company wanted my help and went on to say he ran a rather small company.   And, he actually told me he couldn't say for sure that he had any budget.   If the CEO does not know about his budget, we have a problem.

In larger corporations, poor mouth is used citing limited departmental budgets and any funds that they do have must be stretched until their year-end.

Tip: When exposed to the poor mouth strategy let your profitability and cost modeling become your guide.   Don't get drawn in by all of the false theatrics. Remember, when we negotiate in good faith we must be allowed to be profitable. Otherwise, we are being used.

10.   Buyer Creates "Beat the Clock" Scheme

In 2007 when the financial markets started to crack, the retail and manufacturing markets gradually switched from a seller's market to buyer's market.   Part of the change was the financial piece. Part of it was the velocity of the internet and consumer friendly database software.   And, part of it was the understanding by buyers that there were too many sellers and not enough buyers.   The buyers were truly in the driver's seat after a long respite and they were becoming aggressive.

The result has been the emergence of a lethal negotiation strategy that we at Centroid Training refer to as "Beat the Clock".   This strategy by name alone tells us that it is a time compression negotiation strategy with most of the risk and financial exposure placed on the seller.   Here's how it works.   The buyer calls the seller and says, "I have a large budget that must be spent quickly.   I need the best deal you can conjure up in the next few minutes. If you cannot satisfy my needs I will move on to the next supplier in your region who is hungrier than you." The buyer has prepared her/himself in advance of the call with all rate structures known in the market for your products and that of your competitors. The best time to execute this strategy by the buyer is later in the day. This places the maximum pressure on the seller to make a decision that the buyer will accept or the seller faces losing that precious customer expenditure.

Tip: If we know that "Beat the Clock" is being used with regularity by an aggressive customer or group of customers (think 3rd party agents) we must change our behavior to soften the effects of this pressure cooker negotiation strategy. This means we must get better at keeping rate history and profitability thresholds within arms reach at all times. It means our cost modeling must be sound and profitable. If we are wise, we will also perform a mini SWOT analysis of this customer's company and our company. The result will be that no matter how quick and pressured the buyer makes us feel, we stand a much better chance of staying profitable. We do not want to erode our entire business.

11.   The Auction Strategy

You could use the following negotiation for almost any large ticket purchase where there are several sales outlets or channels for an identical product. This example was exactly how I negotiated the purchase of my last new car and saved approximately 7% on asking price.

We use time compression to our advantage in this negotiation strategy.

In the auction strategy automobile example, we visit three car dealerships knowing exactly what model and features we want. We advise the salesperson that we are going to buy a car within 24 hours. We also tell them we are going to visit two other car dealerships and no "offer" details between the other car dealers will be shared.

We request their best price now, but we request that they remain profitable in formulating their deal. Once the three dealership offers are submitted to us, the losing bids will be called and told they did not succeed. That's all. The winning dealership gets the congratulatory call, and we sign the deal.

Tip: You cannot bluff on the purchase of the high ticket item or you will lose all credibility. Secondly, it is absolutely essential that you know exactly what model and exactly what features you want on the product you are purchasing because if there is any variance in the product being compared the auction approach loses its effect.

12.   The Burden of Proof Strategy

You would not normally think of "Burden of Proof" as a negotiation strategy, but let me assure you it is, and it can be a very effective bargaining instrument. The burden of proof is widely used in many segments of business as a way to mitigate risk. If a buyer or seller makes a claim, the other side can simply call them on it and ask for proof of the claim.

There are circumstances where burden of proof can be used to weigh the other side down in a negotiation by asking for copious amounts of information to defend a position. Burden of proof when applied all at once with tight deadlines (time compression) pressures the other side into making quick decisions. If the side being asked to prove a claim cannot produce the information requested, this will cast a shadow of doubt, and on occasion, create downward pressure on price.

It can also be used by the average consumer when buying a house. A smart purchaser of homes typically has a home inspection done of the property before the deal closes to uncover any irregularities with the property. Hiring an experienced home inspector is smart. Another avenue and not often undertaken, involves hiring a person who has personally build homes or who has professionally made a living as a tradesperson such a plumber or electrician. Why you ask? It has to do with the billions of dollars in home renovation that has taken place worldwide in the past two decades. Improving our homes has been a way to grow wealth at a reasonable cost. The burden of proof revolves around home improvements adhering to building and health code. I can't tell you how many times work not done to code has saved me from not buying a home or better yet has helped me claw back thousands and thousands of dollars on the price of a home in the negotiation stage.

In one particular case, my family was interested in buying an older home that had been heavily renovated at a cost of just under $200,000 in improvements. We toured the house and it was immaculate. Finally, with my construction associates we decided to look at the basement. The basement was unfinished but it was as clean as a whistle. It was so clean that the owner saw fit to take out a wall in the middle of the basement. The bad news was that the wall in question was a supporting wall for the whole house. Worse yet, the owner had not replaced the missing wall with structural jacks to hold the house up. The cost to bring this house back up to code was substantial. Needless to say, we declined to close the deal.

Tip: Building and health codes are a constantly evolving set of codes so enlist building inspectors or tradespeople who are current and experts in this field. Asking calm questions about construction code is not meant to be confrontational. It is smart.

Finally, as a seller, after reviewing the above burden of proof negotiation strategy examples, look at your business environment and ask yourself how can I use this information in my next sales negotiation? Think customer budget commitments, contract signing, product trials and business consolidation at the expense of your sales competitors!

STRATEGY SUMMARY

The 12 buyer strategies I have shared with you are being used by your customers on an hourly and daily basis. Therefore, it is in your best interest to sharpen your negotiation game and learn to identify these strategies early in negotiations. Learn to neutralize them or reroute them into a less competitive and more interest based channel. What makes all of the above strategies even more effective and compelling is that buyers are using these strategies by phone, e-mail, and Skype. This means that as a seller, you are losing more and more face-time with your customers. This means you do not have the ability to read your negotiation partner's face and body movements so critical to understanding how stressed or how serious they really are. It says to me, we must raise our game. We must do our best to pull game theory based negotiations toward more amicable interest based negotiations where both parties are permitted to be profitable. We want strong, smart, relationship based deals that stand the test of time.

FINAL THOUGHTS

Sales negotiation is eternally and constructively tied to consultative selling. So we must always be very mindful of the power and strength of long-term trusting businesses relationships. Armor-piercing questions in their various forms must not be seen as anything other than a positive risk tool used to clarify our bargaining position and that of our negotiation partner.

Our personal brand and bargaining table image is nothing more than our personal set of perfectly repeatable promises at work. How we frame negotiations. How we prepare negotiations. How we conduct and manage stratagems.

I hope you now understand after reading this book sales negotiation is a craft comprised of philosophy, theory, and art. Sales negotiation on the ground and at the bargaining table is a game of elasticity. It is a plethora of plans and back-up plans (BATNA) that lead us into a profitable bargaining continuum.

Preparation cannot be understated. To be a truly great sales negotiator, you must be able to digest all known facts about any negotiation well enough to un-script in the heat of a bargaining exchange to elevate your cause and claim greater value. Our knowledge of strategy and our ability to shift strategy in the blink of an eye makes us a force to be reckoned with.

Remember, the world of sales negotiation is a fluid environment. We must continue to add new tools to our negotiation repertoire. Read, practice, and implement bravely.

Be creative. Offer great value. Make friends. Be true to yourself.

Here's hoping we meet one day across a bargaining table. Here's hoping we shake hands over a profitable deal that will stand the test of time.

ACKNOWLEDGEMENTS

I cannot imagine writing a book in total isolation.

This long list of people helped, pushed, pulled, cajoled, and cheered me on as I discovered *Unlocking Yes* deep inside me.

Please accept my gratitude:

Steve Cosic	Steve MacFarlane
Randy Craig	Glenn Marshall
Bob & Peggy Duck	Debra Rother
Don Fisher	Ken Smith
Katie Fullerton	Mark Spencer
Bryan Hamilton	Ellie Stutsman
Doug & Marg Hall	David Titcombe
Chris Kata	…..to mention a few.
David Kingsmill	

A special thank you to Mark Spencer who kept saying over and over again "Pat you have to get all of this negotiation knowledge written in a book."

Also a special thank you to Glenn Marshall and The Greening Marketing Team for their expert knowledge on publishing and cover design.   Smart people executing on what they do best.

REFERENCES

Although I did not directly quote any other published negotiation book sources, I did refer to and take inspiration from the following list of fine authors on Creativity, Consultative Selling, Strategy & Negotiation.

Edward de Bono. *Six Thinking Hats* 1985, 1999, 2000

David H. Maister, Charles H. Green & Robert M. Galford. *The Trusted Advisor* 2004

Marcus Buckingham & Donald O. Clifton. *Now, Discover Your Strengths* 2001

Sun Tzu. *The Art Of War* 2008

Gavin Kennedy. *Essential Negotiation An A-Z Guide* 2009

Herb Cohen. *You Can Negotiate Anything* 1980, 1981, 1982

Roger Fisher & William Ury. *Getting To Yes Negotiating Agreement Without Giving In* 1981, 1991

Chester L. Karrass. *Give and Take The Complete Guide to Negotiating Strategies and Tactics* 1974, 1993

Tony Fang. *Chinese Business Negotiating Style* 1999

George H. Ross. *Trump Style Negotiation Powerful Strategies And Tactics For Mastering Every Deal 2006*

Leigh Thompson. *The Truth About Negotiations* 2008

Deepak Malhotra & Max H. Bazerman. *Negotiation Genius How to Overcome Obstacles and Achieve Brilliant Results at the Bargaining Table and Beyond* 2007

Please note all of the above books are "Recommended Reads" by Patrick Tinney, Managing Partner, Centroid Training & Marketing. These books can be purchased through our website at www.centroidmarketing.com

INDEX

A

Appear strong, 119
aspirations/goals, 79

B

back-up plan, 75, 87, 93, 106
bargaining, 1, 10, 11, 14, 15, 16, 27, 33, 34,
    37, 39, 40, 41, 43, 51, 52, 56, 57, 62, 64,
    65, 68, 69, 71, 72, 73, 74, 75, 76, 77, 78,
    79, 80, 82, 83, 84, 87, 91, 92, 93, 102, 106,
    110, 111, 114, 115, 116, 117, 127, 129,
    130, 132, 135, 136, 139, 141, 142, 148,
    151, 152, 153, 165, 168
Bargaining Continuum, 15, 39, 101, 102,
    103, 148
bargaining table, 27, 76, 127
BATNA, 6, 15, 27, 39, 42, 54, 62, 67, 68, 75,
    77, 80, 84, 87, 92, 93, 94, 108, 127, 137,
    160, 168
BATNA (Best Alternative To A Negotiated
    Agreement), 6, 27
benefits, 9, 97, 132, 149, 159, 97
Big Money, 83
bigger-piece-of-the-pie negotiator, 1
body language, 20, 37, 68, 69, 71, 84, 92, 152
Brand Alignment, 42
Budget information, 31
Budget Pressures, 83
Budgets, 48, 70
Build partnerships, 119
Business external, 11
Business internal, 11
Business Negotiation, 1, 17

C

capital expenditure, 4
Cascade/contagion price erosion, 77
Cash Is King, 48
Close smart deals, 6
collaboration, 9, 61, 74, 75, 139, 152, 153
collaborative, 7, 15, 16, 71, 80, 82, 84

commoditized, 8, 66, 95, 157
Competition, 146
competitive challenges, 5
conflict, 27, 73, 74, 75
consultative selling, 1, 7, 8, 9, 96, 168
content of deal, 130
contract content, 88
Control, 92, 124, 130
Corporate culture, 31
Cost modeling, 15, 87, 94, 123, 113
Cost offsets for both, 40
Creativity, 43, 67, 136, 170
Credibility, 135
curiosity, 30, 80
customer engagements, 5
Customers and trust, 8

D

decompressing time, 64
Demand, 145
Detail, 20, 126
Determination, 117
Disciplined Listening, 36

E

E.Q. skills, 67
Edward de Bono, 67, 170
effectiveness, 68, 73
Emotional intelligence, 20
empathy, 20, 46, 47, 50, 52, 64, 68, 80, 148
Empathy, 96
Ethics/values, 77
expectation gap, 46, 87, 133, 141, 148

F

Family negotiations, 12
finely crafted questions, 13
Framing Sales Negotiations, 115

G

Goal pricing, 130
Goals, 31
growth expectations, 5

H

Handle objections, 74
handling objections, 6, 95
Hidden value, 146
High Value Questions, 30
History, 116

I

I.Q. skills, 67
Innovation, 43, 145
Inquisitiveness, 19

K

Killer instinct, 21
knowledge, 12, 37, 39, 53, 118, 146, 148, 157, 168, 169

L

Large personal purchases, 11
Leaky Strategies, 107
Limited Strategies, 112
Listen, 62, 84, 96
Listen and acknowledge, 84
Listen to them, 62
Lose/Lose, 17
Lose/Win, 17

M

Managing Risk, 129
Market share erosion, 58
Marketing, 63, 101, 169, 170
Mental agility, 20
mini SWOT Analysis, 6
Mobile, Skype or e-Mail, 122, 124

Money Questions, 74

N

Need, 14, 22, 24, 155
negative risk, 14, 26, 33, 66, 83, 86, 91, 111, 129, 136, 142, 148
negotiation philosophy, 14
Negotiation Strategies, 111, 154, 155
negotiation table, 14, 51, 53, 62, 66, 71, 84, 93, 126, 135, 136
Negotiator Traits, 19
New markets, 55, 58
New product development, 55, 58
New product launches, 58
New technology, 55, 58
No, 16, 23, 24, 35, 37, 96, 133, 136, 148, 159, 163
Note takers role, 124

O

Objectives, 15, 45, 75, 91
Offer value, 63

P

philosophy, 10, 14, 15, 16, 17, 91, 168
Planned meeting objectives, 37
Post Mortem, 151
power calls, 5
Preparation, 54, 123, 135, 168
Price, 44, 94, 144, 156
Problem resolution response times, 56
process, 3, 1, 6, 10, 13, 14, 15, 20, 21, 22, 25, 26, 37, 44, 49, 62, 65, 67, 68, 73, 74, 91, 95, 96, 97, 109, 116, 119, 135, 136, 141, 148, 149, 152
procurement processes, 1
professional buyers, 1, 64
Professional negotiators, 10, 13, 75, 87, 114
Profile of negotiators, 41
Profit erosion, 58
profitable closure, 1
profitable deal, 14, 46, 168

Proposal incentives, 93

Q

Quality, 44, 56, 94, 144
quantitative easing, 5
queries, 54, 56, 64, 73, 86, 123, 141, 152
Query, 96

R

Ranked high value questions, 37
Ranked objectives, 123
Reconnaissance, 15, 39, 113
Reduce Conflict, 73
relationship business, 5
relationship-based selling, 1
Relationships, 5, 49, 60, 64
Rephrase, 96
Reputation, 12, 135
Response expectations, 31
Risk assessment, 20

S

Sales negotiation, 1, 6, 104, 168
Sales Negotiation Tactics, 104
Sales Negotiation Traps, 86
Sales Objections, 95
sales professionals, 1
Scarcity, 118
Scripting, 132
Sell futures, 120
Shared business economics, 40
Show leadership, 119
Show up, 63
Situational analysis, 113
Six Thinking Hats, 67, 68, 170
smartly-crafted business deals, 16
Solving problems, 65
Spirit of agreement, 116
spirit of the deal, 148
Statistics Canada, 18
Stay in the present, 37, 71
Storytellers, 20

Storytelling, 78, 79
Strategic alliances, 55
Strategic purchases, 58
Strategy, 6, 7, 9, 19, 68, 91, 110, 132, 158, 159, 161, 163, 164, 165, 167, 170
Succeed with deeds, 62
Supercharge, 25
Supply, 56, 145
Supply chain bottlenecks, 56
SWOT Competitors, 54

T

Table presence, 136
Tactical responses, 91
Tactics, 14, 104, 152, 170
Technology, 36, 44, 56, 58
tells, 111
The Auction, 99, 164
The Buyers Market, 48
Time awareness, 20
time compression, 5, 39, 98, 99, 111, 123, 136, 155, 156, 159, 163, 164, 165
Time Decompression, 98, 99
Timing, 31, 44, 111, 139
Trial close, 97, 139
Trial Closes, 138, 139
Trust, 8, 23, 24, 60, 61, 62, 63, 80

U

Unique points of difference, 58
unique propositions, 50
Uniqueness, 145
Un-Scripting, 132
Using a note taker, 37

V

Value Statements, 141
visualization, 80, 90

W

walk away, 49, 87, 96, 130, 148

walk away position, 87
Win a little extra, 17
Win/Lose, 16, 17, 103
Win/Win, 16, 17, 27, 75, 158
Wise Deals, 50
Women In Business, 125

Y

Yes, 1, 2, 17, 22, 23, 24, 139, 155, 156, 169, 170

Z

ZOPA or Zone of Potential Agreement, 15, 102

NOTES

NOTES

CPSIA information can be obtained
at www.ICGtesting.com
Printed in the USA
LVHW042112081218
599749LV00025BA/433/P

9 780993 828416